THE CRUCIBLE
OF GLOBAL WAR

CHRISTOPHER PETITT
THE CRUCIBLE OF GLOBAL WAR

And the Sequence that is Leading Back to It

RockCreek
PUBLISHING, LLC

The Crucible of Global War
And the Sequence that is Leading Back to It

Christopher Petitt

F I R S T E D I T I O N

Hardcover ISBN: 978-1-942545-28-6
Paperback ISBN: 978-1-942545-34-7
eBook ISBN: 978-1-942545-35-4

Library of Congress Control Number: 2015954875

RockCreek
PUBLISHING, LLC

Rock Creek Publishing, LLC
An Imprint of Wyatt-MacKenzie

For the youth of the Y and Z Generations and,
of whom, I am especially fondest:
Chris, Jared & Jordan, Eden & John.
Your celebrations will be indelible; expect nothing less.

CONTENTS

The silence spreads. I talk and must talk. So I speak to him and say to him: "Comrade, I did not want to kill you. If you jumped in here again, I would not do it, if you would be sensible too. But you were only an idea to me before, an abstraction that lived in my mind and called forth its appropriate response. It was that abstraction I stabbed. But now, for the first time, I see you are a man like me. I thought of your hand-grenades, of your bayonet, of your rifle; now I see your wife and your face and our fellowship. Forgive me, comrade. We always see it too late. Why do they never tell us that you are poor devils like us, that your mothers are just as anxious as ours, and that we have the same fear of death, and the same dying and the same agony — forgive me, comrade; how could you be my enemy? If we threw away these rifles and this uniform you could be my brother, just like Kat and Albert. Take twenty years of my life, comrade, and stand up — take more, for I do not know what I can even attempt to do with it now."

—Paul Bäumer in *All Quiet on the Western Front*,
by Erich Maria Remarque

PROLOGUE

In May of 2012, I was fortunate to be in Washington D.C. attending my daughter's graduation from George Washington University. Other schools were holding commencement exercises the same week – American and Georgetown, in particular – and the hotels and restaurants of the city were festive and full of enthusiastic, spirited kids and their parents, siblings, and, as in the case of my daughter, grandparents. It was a time and place of hope and idealism and looking forward. These kids, this nation's future, were set to go forth in the world and make it their own.

At the graduation ceremony, former NBC news anchor Brian Williams and Mexican business magnate Carlos Slim gave motivational addresses to the graduates. We watched, my parents and I, from our seats on the National Mall, the Smithsonian to our side, the Capitol building behind us, and the Washington Monument and Lincoln Memorial ahead in the distance. It was a warm spring day, and the scene was inspirational. No doubt the graduates felt promise and optimism in the air.

And yet, I couldn't shake a nagging feeling of despair for them. Gnawing at me all week was the theory that had been forming in my mind, a theory I had begun to contemplate seriously just a couple of years prior. After the housing crash of 2007, the world had become a different place, economically at the very least. Having been in the investment business, a participant of the very start of the hedge fund industry, I had had a unique vantage point from which to watch things unfold. My business – my livelihood – dealt with financial risk, and I probably understood the gravity of the situation better than most.

But to my mind it was more than this, more than just the economics. The world was changing. I sensed it, even if I didn't have a real handle on what it was that I sensed. By 2009, I knew I had to better define it. My career depended on it. I needed to understand the trends, where the markets – and the world – were heading. The problem was, there were too few clues. Businesses were wallowing, the markets were floundering, and the economy was not heading in any identifiable direction.

And so I began to look backwards instead of forwards. How did we get here in the first place? I went back, decade by decade, my study of the economic course of the world becoming fueled more by obsessive curiosity than by career necessity. By 2010, I was studying the Great Depression and the parallels stopped me in my tracks. The similarities in the years leading to the Great Depression and the current years were striking. Was it a coincidence, or was there a genuine connection? And if the latter, were these two periods of time, however connected, unique unto themselves? Were they just two isolated, yet related, events of history?

I went back further. Four or five generations prior to the Great Depression, similar events had played out globally just before the American Civil War and a series of other wars around the world. And four or five generations before that, the same. And four or five generations before that. A theory began to formulate in my mind.

My career had been put on hold and for three years I researched and studied and explored the theory. The final draft you now hold in your hands. I trust it will be found to be thought-provoking, perhaps creating a pause in the shared conviction of many. Major historical developments over the last half millennium point to a seemingly undeniable sequence, a rhythm of humankind with one very glaring recurring event: global warfare. If the sequence holds – and for the reasons conveyed herein, I submit that it cannot do otherwise – the world will likely see massive war, the kind that comes about once a century, the kind that touches all corners of civilization, the kind that changes everything.

The theory is either prescient or a false alarm and the reader must determine which. I hesitated over my findings, hesitated over just what to do with them. I knew that if I kept them to myself, I could avoid the criticism and controversy this book might engender. Alarmist, war-obsessed, doomsayer – these were the labels I imagined being affixed to me, none of which could be further from the truth. Friends and relatives tend to describe me as a rational, analytical-minded, fairly unassuming, optimistic guy with middle-of-the-road political beliefs. But I'm also a patriot with a deep love for my country and an even deeper concern for what I believe lies ahead for her. In the end, I decided I needed to share my theory as a warning. I felt an obligation to at least put my thoughts out there for discussion and debate, and maybe even to have my theory proved wrong (which would be to my great relief). A tragic storm is brewing, and I determined I could not sit idly and quietly with what my research had uncovered and my experience was telling me. "The hottest places in hell," John F. Kennedy said, "are reserved for those who, in times of great moral crisis, maintain their neutrality."

The pages that follow are, of necessity, broad in scope. There is history, there is economics, there is human psychology, there is philosophy, there is common sense. The sequence of events that inevitably leads to global war cuts across all these disciplines. There is geography and there is politics as well, mostly revolving around the West, for it is the West that is dominant in the geopolitical world order of today (but may or not be in the world order of tomorrow; time will tell). My understanding of economics, my analytical background, my lifelong love of history and politics, my travel throughout Europe, Asia, and the Middle East – all have, I hope, provided me with sufficient background to communicate my thoughts effectively. This is not meant to be an academic treatise. I offer this book to the general reader in the hope that it will be understood for what I intend it to be – above all else, a challenge to face the future, no matter how grim it might be.

In Washington, D.C. for my daughter's graduation, I took my parents to see some of the monuments, the World War II Memorial in particular. My parents are a part of this nation's Greatest Generation and the significance was not lost on me when, that very weekend, we attended the commencement exercises and watched the latest generation preparing to take the torch and enter into a time of history that will see turmoil of the scale their predecessors saw. This was the moment I could not shake my nagging despair. In my mind, I could not help but connect the two generations, and in the cheerful faces of the young graduates, I could imagine the faces of those who came some seventy-five years before, at a time when the world was just beginning to fall apart – when the unthinkable was still unthinkable. They, too, possessed a youthful exuberance. And they, too, would be tested in unimaginable ways, their youth dying on the vine in the darkness of war. But replaced, in the course of their obligation – to each other, to their nation, to the future of the world as they saw it – by resolve and determination and monumental sacrifice.

I watched as my daughter and her classmates turned their tassels and I felt heartened by the idea, one that I firmly believe, that the worst of times brings out the best in humankind. Perhaps I was surveying the next Greatest Generation. The course forthcoming will require rising above self-interest; it will require an ability to act boldly, to not wobble indecisively down paths of least resistance. It will require a sense of what is truly at stake. It will require greatness. Facing a world again torn asunder may well be the destiny of this young generation. And as with the World War II generation, their collective response will define their legacy.

As the coming years unfold, the challenge will become more urgent. The call will become louder. We must – all of us – be ready. The world is changing, and the changing will be brutal. The clues of history are plain to see, as I hope to make clear to you in the pages that follow. History – relentlessly, inevitably – is preparing to repeat itself.

—November, 2015

CHAPTER ONE

The Order of Things

In all chaos there is a cosmos, in all disorder a secret order.
CARL JUNG

It wasn't supposed to be like this.

When the Soviet Union fell in 1991, one lone superpower remained standing. The United States had won the Cold War. The world was safe for democracy. The world was safe, period. American values had been upheld, vindicated, cheered, and embraced.

The rest of the decade reflected the ebullient mood of a world that had seemingly conquered history itself. The 1990s were years of peace and prosperity for most of the world. Markets grew far beyond national boundaries. Economic institutions like the World Trade Organization and legislation like the North American Free Trade Agreement helped usher in the liberalization of international commerce. Economies grew not only in the First World countries, but also in the emerging ones throughout Asia, Eastern Europe, and the Middle East. And the rise in the United States was nothing less than stunning. Incomes rose, wealth rose, and dot-com technology companies helped lead the Dow from 2,633 at the end of 1990 to 11,723 by the beginning of 2000 – a staggering 345% increase, representing, maybe better than anything, the optimism of the age. Times were good, and as the decade rolled on, the most serious national news story was a sex scandal in the White House. A presidential fling with an intern was what grabbed America's attention.

Meanwhile, the rise of the Internet brought everybody closer, leading the way towards the rise of unparalleled globalization, and not just economically. The sharing of music and art and culture went worldwide with hardly a region of the globe unaffected. The world became a smaller place with more shared interests. Indeed, "It's a Small World" became one of the most popular attractions at the new Euro Disney just outside of Paris, to which more people traveled than to the city of Paris itself. People could buy Big Macs from Morocco to Belarus. The world was connected. There was a hopeful buoyancy and a sense that we were all (finally) on the same page, or at least headed that way.

All of this ended, of course, on a September day in 2001. Americans were introduced to other parts of the world, other cultures, other concerns. Osama bin Laden and al-Qaeda became household names. The optimism faded. The dot-com bubble burst. Globalization suddenly meant more than just taking in the good. Globalization meant taking it all in. It meant becoming exposed to all of the world's dangers. A small world with pervasive cultural influences meant far-reaching, often unintended, and uncontrollable consequences. Globalization came with baggage.

"Right Here, Right Now" by Jesus Jones, a popular song of the '90s, talked of watching the world wake up from history. The song got it exactly wrong. The 1990s offered a respite from history. The West napped through the decade while history played itself out as it always has. Since 9/11, the world has become a dangerous, volatile place. In the Middle East, terrorist groups like al-Qaeda continue to proliferate. There is Hamas and Hezbollah, new household names. The Islamic State of Iraq and Syria (ISIS) continues to threaten the region, operating in the Sinai Peninsula, Libya, North Africa, South Asia, and Southeast Asia. The price of oil has plummeted and the economies of Middle Eastern nations are in shambles. There are uprisings and civil wars in several countries. Syria has broken apart. The age-old conflict between the Shias and the Sunnis throughout the Middle East has reached an unprecedented level of intensity.

In Eastern Europe, there is concern over nations that used to be a part of the fallen superpower – the old Soviet bloc. Russian expansion into Eastern Europe and Asia Minor is strikingly reminiscent of a Cold War that was already waged and supposedly decided. In the South China Sea, there are disputes between China and a host of countries, including the Philippines, Malaysia, Taiwan, and Vietnam. There are disputes among China, South Korea, and Japan as well, not to mention the intermittent bluster from North Korea.

Everywhere, there are signs of economic stagnation. Japan wobbles in and out of recession. The Chinese economic powerhouse has stumbled. The euro is in crisis and global financial inequality is at its highest level since the Great Depression. Reluctant to commit to growth-generating capital investments, massive multinational corporations and the world's ultra-rich accumulate wealth at an alarming rate, far exceeding historical norms.

In the U.S. in particular, the economic recovery is sluggish and uneven at best. We are told that brighter economic times have returned and the stock market is pointed to as evidence of a presumably growing economy. But in the meantime, consumer spending is weak as the unconvinced populace hangs onto its money. The sense is that U.S. gains have come mostly by way of government stimulus plans financed with unsustainable debt and central bank easy-money policies. How long can the propping-up go on?

Everyday Americans can see that middle-class career opportunities are more elusive than ever as the once-industrialized economy continues its shift toward lower-paying service sectors. Technology is displacing workers and outsourced manufacturing jobs have yet to return. Will they ever? Students earn degrees – even MBAs – and spend their postgraduate days in minimum-wage jobs. Interest rates are low but housing affordability continues to slip further away for most people.

If U.S. economic stimulus comes at the cost of unsustainable debt, it comes also at a cost to foreign economies. At a glance, what might look promising – the economy of the U.S. – upon serious reflection seems to be an anomaly in global financial terms. Economies are stagnating in Europe, Japan, China, Russia, and seemingly everywhere else. Nowhere are things as bad as they are in the Middle East. The glut of oil means low prices at the gas pumps in the West, but it means devastated – and dangerous – economies throughout the nations that supply most of the world's fuel.

Ineffective long-term economic policy is met with ineffective long-term geopolitical policy. Political indecisiveness now marks the direction of the world. Organizations such as NATO and the United Nations seem helpless, if not anachronistic. The United States, meanwhile, that bastion of democracy and capitalism that won the Cold War, has sunk into malaise and weakness of leadership. Respected U.S. potency has fallen into resented American hegemony.

All in all, the world seems a muddling, rudderless place, even chaotic. Even before the fall of the Soviet Union, it was never quite like this. The fifties and sixties and seventies and eighties had their moments, to be sure, but behind the sporadic crises, there was always some sense of stability. The order of the world seemed steady and predictable. The Cold War had been something that could be counted on; the enemy a known threat. What happened to that order? Why has it seemingly fallen away? More importantly, why now?

As World War II ended, an age of relative peace and prosperity began, ushering in the Space Age which dovetailed into the Digital Age. Huge technological advances made for a better standard of living and kept the economic engine of the world humming. The two main powers of the world, the U.S. and U.S.S.R., kept each other in check and the rest of the world fell in line behind them. This "Superpower" world order provided a level of stability that contrasted sharply with the state of the world just prior to the War. In fact, at the beginning of the twentieth century, the world began to enter into a period of volatility that now seems eerily familiar. The volatility was marked by dangerous geopolitical hotspots, global economic stagnation, financial inequality, and a general lack of order and direction. In a few short decades, the world would see one "Great" depression as well as two world wars.

Interestingly, the volatility at the beginning of the last century was also preceded by a long period of relative peace and prosperity. Standards of living around the world rose in the latter half of the nineteenth century and people lived well. There was war – there is always war somewhere – but it was limited in scope and never really threatened the world at large. During those years, great nations arose. A loose confederation of states united itself under Otto Von Bismarck to form a powerful Germany. Other European countries consolidated power, too. The United States stretched across a continent. It was an age of Nationalism and, like the Superpower order that followed, it provided stability. There was a steadiness and predictability.

But Nationalism didn't just appear out of nowhere. It, too, had been forged in a period of great instability. 1848 marked the Year of Revolution across Europe. Germany rose through the Prussian wars. The Crimean War strengthened the Ottomans and empowered France in particular. The United States expanded, but only on the heels, and as a result of, the Civil War. This period of conflict, as the one that would follow in the twentieth century, began before the shots were fired and had all the usual symptoms: general global discord, economic malaise, directionless leadership.

And before that volatility? Another era of relative peace and prosperity. The late eighteenth century leading into the first half of the nineteenth century was marked by another period wherein standards of living rose, people lived well, and the world was generally defined by steadiness and pre-dictability. This was the age that followed the American and French revolutions, and the Napoleonic Wars. It was an age of representative government, an age of "self-determination," but an age that, like the others, was born in volatility, namely the revolutions, although there was conflict elsewhere as well.

Yet another age of progress preceded that. The Age of Discovery saw the spread of civilization to places previously unknown. Empires were built, and those empires were directed by the absolute rule of monarchs. Like the Superpower world order, the world order of Nationalism, and the world order of Self-Determination, this order of Absolutism was also marked by stability and consistency. And it, too, came in on a wave of volatility, unseating through war an order of the world that had been defined largely by the Church following the Dark Ages, which, in turn, had come on the heels of the fall of the Roman Empire.

What does this all mean? Among other things, it means that in terms of volatility, we are not exactly in unchartered waters. Although people always seem to consider the times they live in to be unique, perhaps they are not so unique after all. History appears to show the experience of humankind proceeds in a repeated series: good times (progress, advancement, relative peace), volatility (discord and danger), bad times (conflict that is global in scope), and then good times again.

Note that this describes much more than a world simply enduring random ups and downs. There is very little that is random in this pattern and the pattern seems to hold consistently throughout history. There is a definable sequence to it. That is to say that good times are never followed by more good times. There is always an interruption. And after the dust settles on world-altering global conflict, we don't backslide into volatility. And global war never comes unless it is immediately preceded by a volatile period. It is – always – progress and peace, discord and danger, conflict and war. In that sequence.

Definitive periods going back some four centuries can be more or less summarized like so:

World Order	Approximate Time Frame
Absolutism	1648-1776
Self-Determination	1776-1850s
Nationalism	1850s-1945
Superpowers	1945-

Undeniably, each of these periods coincided with a significant phase of human advancement, a time of great technological progress. By the late 1600s, for example, the Renaissance had spawned the Scientific Revolution. Traditional doctrines of church dogma were replaced by significant developments in the fields of astronomy, physics, and mathematics. The earth was flat no longer, nor was it at the center of the universe. Newton advanced his law of universal gravitation, and science gave the world a new outlook on nature and our place in it. Meanwhile, the Age of Discovery had been in full swing, giving rise to the exploration and colonization of the Americas (as well as Africa and Asia), ultimately leading to a new geopolitical order of empires and a period of great economic productivity marked by mercantilism; empires exploited the resources of the colonies that they controlled.

Roughly a century later, accompanying the age of Self-Determination, a new era of productivity came along. Advances in manufacturing processes with the rise of machines – James Watt's steam engine directing the charge – led to the period that would become known as the Industrial Revolution.

Another century came and went. Another geopolitical order took the world stage. During the era of Nationalism came another age of world-changing advancement. Widespread application of technology brought electrification and the internal combustion engine. The way people communicated took a momentous leap, first with the telegraph, then the telephone, and eventually the radio. Iron became steel and the machines that were powered by steam were now powered by electricity as mass production transitioned to the assembly line. Railroads carried people and goods from one end of a country to another. Oil began to fuel the world. It became known as the Second Industrial Revolution. Then, a century later, humankind's progress was marked by the Space-Digital Age.

Note the connection between the geopolitical order of the day and the period of human progress:

Major Advancement Periods and World Orders: 1700-Now

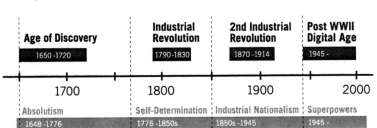

With each significant rise in progress, however, came an equally significant fall. At the tail end of the Age of Discovery and its economic system of mercantilism, there were credit crises, panics, and government defaults. The same happened at the end of the First Industrial Revolution. Market panics came along like clockwork in 1837, 1847, and 1857. The Second Industrial Revolution would end with nothing less than the Great Depression. In each case, the long era of productive growth came crashing down into global economic collapse.

And then, in each case, things got worse. Every time, the world experienced a climate of chaos, a general state of confusion resulting from the lack of any recognizable authority, a sense of ineffectiveness. In each case, the state of the world moved from order to disorder marked by economic stagnation, strained international relations, domestic political divisiveness, and financial imbalances.

Going almost certainly unnoticed by the world's inhabitants towards the end of each order was a series of seemingly unconnected events, the kind of historical events that are only connected in retrospect. The "lead-up" occurred over decades, too slow and gradual for any one generation to realize the significance of where the world was heading. Ultimately, however, climactic events would occur. A period of conflict would ensue, representing a battle between more than just warring nations; it would represent a battle between the status quo and the future, over what was and what would ultimately be. Each time, the resolution would provide the delineation between the world orders that have been inscribed upon history. But each time, that resolution would come in on nothing less than a crescendo of conflict: war, global in scope.

Absolutism ended with the Seven Years' War, the American and French Revolutions, and the Napoleonic Wars. The age of Self-Determination ended with the Crimean War, the American Civil War, the Prussian wars, and the European wars of unification. The age of Nationalism ended with World War I, the Russian Revolution, wars in Japan and China, the Spanish Civil War, and World War II. These three periods of global conflict are notably unlike other periods of general conflict. During these periods, more than 1% – and up to a full 5% – of the population of that part of the world that was at war was wiped out.

The sequence all of this describes, then, would appear to look like this:

The Cycles of Productivity, Financial Crisis, and Global Conflict: 1700-Now

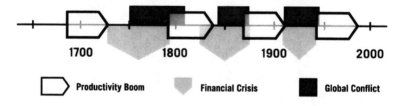

Now, the idea of predictable long-term social and economic cycles that coincide with world order shifts is not entirely new. In 1925, Soviet economist Nikolai Kondratiev noted in his book, *The Major Economic Cycles*, a fifty- to sixty-year historical pattern of booms and busts. His theoretical cycles are now, in fact, known as "Kondratiev waves." Before and since Kondratiev, many notable economists, social scientists, and historians (even Karl Marx, for example) have put forth theories regarding long-term cycles and explanations for why they exist.

The theories abound with controversy. The timing of the supposed cycles – the historical dates of when the cycles start and stop – is debated and even the existence of long-term cycles themselves is in dispute. Many opponents simply chafe at the idea of long-term predictability. A belief in a cyclical pattern of history goes against the grain. It smacks of determinism. It implies a helpless sort of surrender to forces beyond our control. We don't like to think of ourselves as slaves to history. As human beings, we prefer to think of ourselves as makers of history, and on the surface, it seems clear that human affairs don't form predictable patterns. Yes, there are those pesky ups and downs, times of lesser or greater conflict, economic periods of growth and recession, and other such sequences of events that *might* suggest a cyclical structure. But surely these events cannot be said to possess the same kind of knowable regularity or rhythm as, say, spring following winter, the rising and ebbing of the tides, the earth's yearlong trek around the sun, or the annual movement upstream of salmon to spawn. Nature may be somewhat predictable, but with human beings, there's a degree of randomness that can never be accounted for. More than seven billion freewilled spirits walking about the earth must surely guarantee a level of arbitrariness to the world's state of affairs. Unpredictability, it would seem, is simply a part of the human condition. Or so goes the thinking.

Or perhaps the study of cycles has never caught much traction because its importance only comes around once a century or so, with any previous study lost to the institutional memory of the previous period of interest. When things are going well, it is hoped they will continue to do so. No one looks too hard at good times. The bad times seem to garner the most analysis, and the study of cycles seems most prevalent during the chaotic times just prior to a change in world order.

Is the idea of humankind's predictability worth revisiting? To consider that there is an actual sequence of human events that is repeatable (and perhaps inevitable), we must first clear a hurdle or two. If human affairs really do progress in cycles, then looking back over the past five centuries should allow us to see the common elements within the pattern. There should be a connection. We should be able to uncover some-thing significant within these periods that they all share, a sort of inevitability of circumstances that, in the aggregate, forms the cycle. We should be able to, in other words, not only say that human affairs run in cycles, but *why* they do so.

Perhaps most significantly for our time, we should be able to say something meaningful about the future. And about our present – that muddling, rudderless, even chaotic sense of the world in its current state. What does it mean? What *will* it mean?

CHAPTER TWO

Birth of a World Order

There is a mysterious cycle in human events.
To some generations much is given.
Of other generations much is expected.
FRANKLIN D. ROOSEVELT

Joseph Stalin proposed a toast, one of several that night. Accounts differ as to the wording, but it is generally agreed that the toast was for justice, or at least Stalin's view of it. As the toast would make clear, that meant the firing squad for all of the Nazi leaders upon the end of the war. "All 50,000 of them," he said.

Winston Churchill took exception to the toast, according to his memoirs, standing and protesting that "The British Parliament and public will never tolerate mass executions" and adding that he "would rather be taken out into the garden here and now and be shot myself than sully my own and my country's honour by such infamy."

Franklin Delano Roosevelt attempted to introduce some levity into the moment. Suspecting that Stalin was only joking, he suggested a compromise: "How about a smaller number? Say, 49,500?" Everyone was now laughing. Everyone but Churchill.

The toast was made over dinner at the Soviet embassy in Tehran on November 29, 1943. The Tehran conference of the "Big Three" – the U.S., Great Britain, and the Soviet Union – would be followed by conferences in Yalta and Potsdam. The allies would be making huge strategic decisions regarding the prosecution of the war. But the toast and the responses to it are revealing in hindsight. With FDR playing along with Stalin, Churchill was something of the odd man out. This dynamic extended beyond a toast. The conference lasted four days and there are accounts of Stalin and Roosevelt speaking privately, without the presence of Great Britain's prime minister.

The structure of the world's order – its balance of power, its operating code – was changing.

Indeed, history would show that it was Great Britain itself that would become the odd one out. The end of the war revealed two superpowers that the rest of the world more or less aligned with, and Great Britain was not one of them. The new world was quite different from the old world. A mere two decades before, Great Britain could claim authority over one-fifth of the planet's population and almost a fourth of its land area, but by 1945, Great Britain was virtually bankrupt and territories that once belonged to her were falling away.

Who could possibly have foreseen such a development? Well, one person who most likely did was Roosevelt. The world was going to change dramatically, not only as a result of World War II, but also because of the forces of humankind's advancement. FDR almost certainly understood this, and he almost certainly understood not just the changing nature of the world, but the direction of the change. His sidling up to Joseph Stalin was calculated. The Soviets were never going to be an ally in the sense that Great Britain was an ally – with a shared language and heritage – but the Soviets were clearly going to become a major force in the new world. Roosevelt may or may not have been able to anticipate the Cold War that followed, but he undoubtedly anticipated that the U.S.S.R. was going to have a huge say in how a major portion of the world would be governed, and the U.S. would have an even greater say. It was the way in which all the signs were pointing. A new world order was afoot and Roosevelt, knowingly or unknowingly (one must suspect the former), was adroitly navigating his nation into it.

The rise of the superpowers in the postwar years was stunning. Both had obviously proven their military superiority – the U.S. with its technical and industrial might, and the Soviets with their brute and unwavering force. The Americans would be first with the use of atomic weaponry but their arsenal would soon be matched by their former ally. Both nations were riding the technology of the war. The years immediately following would see astounding developments in aircraft technology and rocket science. Technological innovations would include sonar, radar, the development of synthetic rubber and synthetic fuels, huge leaps forward in logistics and navigation, and unparalleled medical advances. Ultimately, the computer, with its roots in the war, would give birth to the digital age.

Bursting onto the global political and economic scenes with the culmination of the war, the Superpower world order had actually been decades in the making. So it is when old orders give way to new. So it was when the world order of Absolutism under the monarchs finally took center stage in the latter Middle Ages, pushing aside an order dominated by the Church, which had slowly stopped working as opportunities began unfolding in the New World. In turn, the era of the monarchs would gradually strain under the pressure applied by the opposing new order of Self-Determination.

The system of the kings' Absolutism slowly began to break down when it could no longer maintain the colonial mercantilism that had been conducive to the developments of the Age of Discovery. Decentralized societies with representative governments emphasizing more individual rights allowed for development in other ways, fostering the Industrial Revolution.

But larger, more central governments would ultimately again be needed to harness the innovations coming from the Industrial Revolution. Self-Determination had been pushed to its limits. Once again, territory had to be unified under common control. Centers of commerce and industry needed to be connected with required resources and energy. Thus, Nationalism became the natural and necessary course of the world, fueling and exploiting the new technologies of the Second Industrial Revolution. The internal combustion engine, electrification, the mass production of steel, the growth of railroads, the assembly line – these were impossible with small, regionalized societies and governments. In time, however, the innovations that were developed during the period of advancement generated by the era of Nationalism would ultimately require a world that would tend towards globalization. The ability of any given nation to advance was limited by its own geopolitical power. Nations, however strong, needed ways by which to expand; the ability to gain influence beyond one's own borders became the dominant objective.

To move beyond national sovereignty, however, was to move towards anarchy. This is the way of things when world orders are tested. Nationalism represented the world's rulebook. It was the embedded status quo, and it worked, as long as the world was in a mode of advancement *within* the boundaries Nationalism made possible. But eventually, the world seemed to grow beyond the status quo. It was as if Nationalism no longer effectively served the world's purpose. The Second

Industrial Revolution began to sputter. Things weren't working like they had before.

The United States experienced the financial panics of 1907 and 1910, which influenced the domestic and global financial markets. In Europe, Germany overtook the British in the industrial production of iron and steel. British and Russian coffers were drained by the Boer War and the Russo-Japanese War, respectively, at the turn of the 20th century, and worker strikes in both countries called for the end of capitalism and the move toward socialism. France went into recession in 1911. The Austrian and Ottoman empires were in the midst of long periods of economic decline. The gap of financial inequality around the world was widening.

The economic turmoil reflected a world moving towards a new but untamed frontier fraught with uncertainty and lacking any strong and common rule of order amongst the world's nations. The rulebook of Nationalism was becoming obsolete, but where was the replacement?

Geopolitically, the anarchy was manifesting itself in a series of conflicts as nations looked, by necessity, for ways to expand. A collection of alliances soon sprang up as an attempt to resolve the defects of the dying world order. The Austro-Hungarian Empire would enter into an alliance with Germany. But this alliance was met in turn by an alliance between Russia and France, both of which had become wary of the militaristic German Empire resting ominously between them. Great Britain allied with France and Belgium, realizing that a German attack across the English Channel would most likely be launched from one of those countries. Other alliances formed throughout Europe as well.

The attempt to expand beyond national sovereignty was catastrophically unsuccessful. World War I ensued with a consequence more devastating than the war itself: the defects of the world went unresolved. Attempts at peace were made postwar with structures like the Treaty of Versailles and the League of Nations, both failures. Anarchy beyond the national sovereign level still reigned.

But with the end of the war in 1918 came the seeds of a new world dynamic. The United States was now a global leader, on her way to becoming a superpower. Although the war brought a dampening effect to certain European economies (Germany's was leveled), the U.S. came out strong and bullish. There was a confidence that permeated the economic landscape. Investment soared, most particularly in the stock market. Share prices rose and rose, and rose some more, mostly on credit. History, of course, tells us that such a boom cannot last. Hope and irrational optimism said otherwise and the result was the Roaring Twenties, a decade that abruptly stopped roaring on October 29, 1929 with the inevitable crash of the stock market. Enter the Great Depression, a period of economic devastation that would last until the start of the next world war.

It was all a sign of Nationalism's demise. But like all the world orders before it, Nationalism did not go quietly. Its end was like a rubber band – the more stretched it is, the more violent the reaction when the band ultimately snaps. For the world, the snapping of Nationalism would be cataclysmic, with a series of revolutions, invasions, and civil wars, all of which would culminate in World War II. For over forty years, the world witnessed an unprecedented level of violence caused by the underlying failures of a world order regulated by Nationalism.

World Conflict from Nationalism 1890-1940

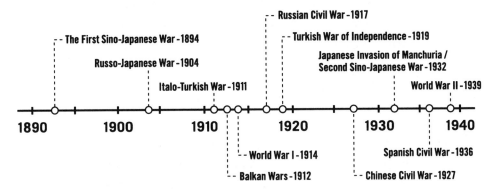

All of this is what FDR, Stalin, and even Churchill understood. This is the context in which the conferences of Tehran, Yalta, and Potsdam were held. A new order of authority was required – a taming of the wild frontier. FDR and Stalin, with the power of their two countries, would provide the direction. Churchill and the dated British Empire not only *would* not, they *could* not. Empires (the German Empire, the Russian Empire, the Imperial Empire of Japan, the Austro-Hungarian Empire, the Ottoman Empire) were relics of the old order.

For the United States, its post-WWII economy skyrocketed. Unemployment was close to 15% before the Second World War but down to 3.8% by 1948. A new era of consumerism took hold. The G.I. Bill provided millions with college educations. Suburbs developed with affordable housing and better modes of transportation. Life was made good by the peaceful and stable environment of the new world order and by the technologies now being exploited.

For the Soviets' part, they expanded as well. But theirs was more of a geographical expansion backed by military force. Soviet satellite countries would come to include Poland,

Romania, Bulgaria, Hungary, and Czechoslovakia. Also coming under Soviet dominance would be Albania, Ukraine, Belorussia, and Yugoslavia, as well as the Baltic states of Estonia, Latvia, and Lithuania.

The development of the Iron Curtain (Churchill's phrase – he never completely lost his impact on geopolitical discourse) created a race for world influence. It was the Cold War, of course, but it was more than this, more than just the standoff that the name "Cold War" implies. What was happening was an active global spreading of geopolitical clout. If the Soviets were spreading their clout in more militaristic ways, the U.S. was spreading theirs by the force of the marketplace. Global markets opened up and technology was helping. Advances in transportation and communications made the whole world more accessible.

What was really happening was that the world was once again finding its way. It had stalled in the era of Nationalism as strong, central governments ventured into fascism and imperialism. Postwar, it picked up again under the direction of the superpowers. The world moved forward. New technologies were born and new resources were exploited. And no resource was as important as oil. It provided the energy to run automobiles, trucks, ships, airplanes, trains, and factories. The development of entire industries (plastics, for example) was made possible because of it. Influence over the Middle East, the world's major cache of oil, would become an integral geopolitical piece of twentieth-century advancement.

What it all led to was the globalization that had been required at the end of the era of Nationalism. It was what Nationalism could not provide. Alliances were made again, but, unlike the pre-World War I alliances, these were forged within the dominance of real authority. Nations were allied with the free world, led by the United States, or they were allied with the power of the Soviet Union. These were alliances that could be counted on, so much so that economically, countries could now afford to outsource. In the old world of Nationalism, a world of questionable alliances, independent self-sufficiency was required, whether it was developed within national boundaries or extended to territories that could be taken by force. But now, nations had trading partners they could reasonably trust. Nations began to specialize and dependencies grew quickly. U.S. farm and industrial lands were turned into suburbs as more and more products were imported. Labor was outsourced, too, starting with lesser tasks like data processing. In time, huge segments of the manufacturing sector would shift abroad to those countries that, in a stabilized environment, could now afford to specialize. The whole world was now following a new rulebook.

This, then, is how world orders are born. They come in by necessity at those critical moments of human history when progress begins to languish. They come in violently, but then they provide not only a new direction for the world but the stability needed for the world's newfound development.

But this presents some questions: Why couldn't Nationalism accommodate the direction of the world? Why did the world have to shift in its geopolitical structure? What makes any given order obsolete, in other words? Why did the order of the Church shift to Absolutism? From Absolutism to Self-Determination? From Self-Determination to Nationalism? What's the common thread? It's as though, from time to time, the framework of the world's power cannot keep up with humankind's advancement. As though it becomes not a nurturing force, but an obstructing one, stifling further progress. And therein lies a clue. Perhaps the larger question is this: What is it that really fuels humankind's advancement?

CHAPTER THREE

Change: The Unstoppable Force of Human Progress

Progress is a nice word. But change is its motivator.
And change has its enemies.
ROBERT F. KENNEDY

On June 26, 1409, the Cathedral of Pisa hosted an extraordinary scene in the remarkable history of the Catholic Church. That day, an elaborate procession moved through the expanse of the magnificent cathedral. Petros Philarghi's coronation as Pope Alexander V would stir controversy that would continue to interest scholars for centuries.

The new pope's procession was stopped three times, whereupon, in each case, the Papal Master of Ceremonies (the title would provide the origin of today's "emcee") would drop to his knees in front of the pope and mournfully voice, "*Sancte Pater, sic transit gloria mundi!*" – Holy Father, so passes worldly glory! It was a reminder to the pope of the fleeting nature of man's world and was especially appropriate for Alexander V, who, in less than a year, would die suddenly from unknown causes (unsubstantiated rumors said he was poisoned by his successor).

The cathedral itself, with its distinctive Pisan Romanesque architecture, would become one of the many iconic images of the Church to this day. Its Corinthian-styled columns, originally crafted for the Great Mosque of Palermo, were wrested away from Islam in the eleventh century. The opulence of its ceilings, adorned with the commissioned mosaics of early Renaissance artists depicting Christ, the Blessed Virgin, and St. John the Evangelist, may have even overshadowed the majesty of the new pope's installment. Pisa's great cathedral is even said to have influenced Galileo in forming his theory of pendulums and the earth's movement by his later observation of the swinging of the immense incense lamp hanging from the center of the cathedral's main nave.

What makes Alexander's papal coronation most interesting is that it took place in Pisa and not Rome as one would expect, and at a time when there was already a pope in place. In fact, there were two. Indeed, it had been the Council of Pisa's idea to elect Philarghi as a means by which to heal the rift that had developed in the Catholic Church between Rome (and eastern parts of Europe) and the Kingdom of France (and other western parts of Europe). The Western Schism, as it came to be known, created the two popes: Gregory XII of Rome and Benedict XIII of Avignon. The Council's solution was to unseat them both and elect a third – Philarghi. But the Council went officially unrecognized by the larger Church and, not surprisingly, was condemned by the supporters of the other popes (a friend of Benedict's called it "a conventicle of demons"). In time, the Catholic Church would officially relegate Alexander to the less-than-flattering category of "antipope," where he sits to this day. But for a short while, the Council of Pisa had effectively produced a third pope.

The divide between Eastern and Western Christendom was more geopolitical in nature than theological. It was, in its essence, a struggle for power. Though resolved in 1418 by the Council of Constance (a single pope – Pope Martin V – replaced the trio of popes), the struggle was part of a larger one taking place throughout Europe and the near East, which would have ramifications throughout the known world. As dissension mounted within the Church, its power was under assault by external forces, as well. Before very long, the monarchs of the day, with power sanctioned and limited by the Church, would come to seek absolute power on their own terms. Part and parcel of the Reformation, the power of a significant portion of the world would shift in the monarch's direction.

History is full of this shifting. So full that it seems undeniably a part of humankind's nature. We are seemingly made to shift, to change, to evolve, to transform. Perhaps nothing is as consistent as the inconsistency of the state of man. Change – the universe's only truly unstoppable force – is guaranteed, and the ritual verse articulated by the Papal Master of Ceremonies in the Cathedral of Pisa on that day in 1409 was intended to remind one of the world's most powerful individuals at the time of that which man understands inherently, yet often forgets in the quest for power: *So passes worldly glory.*

To change, however, is but another way of saying "to create." When there is transformation, something comes into existence that wasn't there before. If we are continuously subject to change, we need look no further than our intrinsic need to create – to produce, to progress, to advance, to better our lot. We bring change upon ourselves. We necessarily, consciously or unconsciously, eschew the confines of what *is*. We are always on the road to *becoming*.

Man creates because man's mind is never idle, at least

for very long. We often create for the sake of creativity. It is a driving force, a means for self-fulfillment. We see it from the time an infant is capable of holding a crayon and it never goes away. People often lose interest in life itself when they reach a point where they can no longer produce, no longer create, no longer feed their inherent compulsion to *make* something.

And we create in order to solve problems. Our environment is constantly changing. Nature is forever transforming and is always just a step ahead of our ability to control her. Our solutions add unforeseen and untold elements into the tangle of our surroundings, producing new problems to solve and rendering the useful life of current creation invariably short. Change is a constant and necessary condition of humankind, and change forces creativity. The two share a symbiotic relationship; not only does change drive creativity, but then, in turn, the new creativity drives further change. It's a perpetual motion machine and an elegant choreography of man and nature. It is good, then, that we are inherently creative and perhaps the inherency is not so accidental. Our survival depends upon it.

On a global, collective level, creativity expresses itself as value-creating production and, in the best case, human progress. Though creativity is continuous, history shows that times of significant progress are often defined by certain eras. The time of the Church was one such era. Coming out of the brutal hardships of the Dark Ages, the Church lit the path for a scarred world, promising redemption for saint and sinner alike and a better world beyond the earthly one for the believer. It gave the world hope and, more importantly, purpose and security. The world once again had leadership and authority under which humankind could operate. What the Church produced was an order – a world order.

By so doing, the Church amassed power, a byproduct of

the era's wealth that was itself a byproduct of the era's creativity. That power may have best been exemplified in 1095, some three hundred years before Philarghi. Pope Urban II made a rousing speech at the Council of Clermont lamenting Muslim control over the Holy Lands. "I, or rather the Lord," spoke Urban, "beseech you as Christ's heralds...to persuade all people of whatever rank...to destroy that vile race from the lands of our friends." A military campaign was thus launched to retake Jerusalem. It became known as the First Crusade and over the course of the next two hundred years there would come half a dozen more, most of which were more about political dominance than theology. Whatever the reasons, the holy wars allowed the Church to consolidate military as well as economic power.

By the 1200s, the Church was in charge of a world that was advancing humankind forward in relative leaps and bounds. What the Church order did, in fact, was lead the world straight towards the Renaissance. But the cultural rebirth of Europe was not necessarily in the Church's long-term best interest. Coming out of the High and Late Middle Ages and into the Renaissance, the intellectual pursuit of philosophical ideas would slowly shift the way in which man saw his place in the universe. By 1543, Copernicus's *De revolutionibus orbium coelestium* (*On the Revolutions of the Heavenly Bodies*) had been published, revealing that the earth was not at the center of the universe as previously believed. This pursuit of ideas kick-started what would become known as the Scientific Revolution, eventually leading to the Age of Enlightenment. From a power standpoint, the Church remained important, but far less relevant. Power began to move towards the monarchs. Authority was still thought to be divinely inspired, but now the inspiration belonged to kings and queens.

This movement had actually been in play for a while.

Over time, the Church's infallibility and divine right to govern had been called into question for a couple of significant reasons. For one thing, the Crusades ended up as an expensive road to nowhere. The Holy Lands remained under Muslim control as part of the Ottoman Empire. And then in the mid-1300s came a terrifying development. People were suddenly becoming ill, stricken with a never-before-seen malady that at first produced tumors, then fever and the vomiting of blood. Within days, maybe a week at the most, came death. The Black Death seems to have originated in Asia, most likely brought to Europe by Genoese traders. However it came, it spread quickly to Italy, France, Spain, Portugal, England, Germany, Scandinavia, Russia, and all points in between.

The plague didn't seem particularly selective about who it victimized. Pious and nonbelievers alike were stricken. Priests were dying as quickly as anybody else – more quickly than they could be replaced. This led to some serious theological questions: Why were the pure of heart dying right alongside the sinners? The Church's answer was to encourage even more piety. The theology was sound; if anything, it just wasn't being practiced as enthusiastically as it should have been. Many, therefore, took to self-flagellation, whipping themselves as a form of penance and purification. But these people died from the plague as well. Eventually, the Church condemned the practice of self-flagellation but the nagging question persisted: Why was the Church powerless to stop the Black Death?

Coming out the Dark Ages, the Church was effective in leading the world order. But eventually, that leadership was questioned – by Luther and the Protestant Reformation, by those who had become cynical of the Crusades, by those contemplating the significance of the Black Death, and by those latching onto new developments in science and intellectual thought. Heading towards the Renaissance, the world was ready to move in new and different ways. The Church, in its medieval form, was slowly becoming a drag on the progress of humankind, and the world reached a crossroads of sorts.

The Church would continue to hold onto its power as best it could in the face of the rapidly changing world. The future was threatening the past and ultimately the direction of the world would be fought for on the battlefield. The ascension of monarchical empires came along with a momentous war. The Thirty Years' War was the single event (if a thirty year process involving a multitude of factions can be called "single"), more than any other, that validated the power of those monarchs setting out on the world's new path.

When a world order operates efficiently, it creates a climate that is conducive to the manifestation of creativity. Grand periods of productivity take place when world orders are in sync with creation. At these moments in time, production pushes humankind forward, creating value and its inseparable byproduct: power. The medieval Church was the most powerful force on Earth since the Roman Empire. But in time – *sic transit gloria mundi* – the power shifted to the kings of England, France, Portugal, Spain, and other monarchies of the world. And for the monarchs, the power was considered absolute. No longer would they be restrained by having to answer to the Pope.

This era of monarchical absolutism, as the era of the Church before it, launched another momentous period of human progress. Discoveries during the Scientific Revolution replaced traditional Church dogma. The world made great leaps in mathematics, physics, astronomy, and biology. Under the monarchs, the Age of Discovery saw the population of the world spread out over the globe. New, previously unconquered frontiers became part of man's dominion and, consequently, the basis for new points of control. Exploration led to the colonization of the New World, catapulting monarchies to empires and leading to the economic system of mercantilism. New intellectual thought from the Age of Enlightenment replaced the ideas of the Church. Thomas Hobbes introduced the idea of the social contract between governments and individuals as a means to move beyond the natural, brute state of man. This legitimized the power of the monarchs (or at least governments in general), but it also helped lead to the idea of individual rights, including property rights. A Protestant work ethic was also developing from the Puritan idea of engagement in hard work as a sign of one's Christian faith.

But the move from the Church order to Absolutism, necessitated by the creative march of humankind, required an unseating of the (failing) status quo. The Thirty Years' War, like the periods of conflict between all the world orders, reveals the painful process of this unseating. Systemic change is always a threat to those empowered by the status quo. People who have come to power through a particular order – a way in which the world works – and who have reaped the attendant wealth of that power, are never prepared to give it up. They'll fight to hang on to it, long past the order's useful life.

But what about the opposing force? What was the motivation for the monarchs to go to war against the Church in the first place? For that matter, what was the motivation for the American revolutionaries, one world order later? Or those seeking stronger, more centralized governments in the new age of Nationalism? What were the motivations of those ushering in the age of the Superpowers? History textbooks, of course, are full of answers specific to the events in question: the pursuit of independence here, the conquest of evil there, the righting of injustices, etc. But do those answers go deep enough? Might there be something more fundamental running beneath the current of each movement – something, perhaps, that they all have in common?

We know that change is inevitable. Humankind's creative impulse guarantees it. But what's behind history's moments of *monumental* change? The kind of change that comes about in nothing less than global war, the kind that always seems to be followed by monumental growth? Man, we know, is a creative being. At the inception of a global order, there is an environment that is conducive to that creativity, an environment conducive to growth and progress. Is it possible, then, that at the end of a world order, man shifts his creative focus to war because his creativity has been somehow stifled by the same order that once cultivated and nurtured it? Is the end of an order, in other words, caused by the loss of the creative environment that originally defined it?

Seen in this light, what really happened, then, from Church to monarch was not only a shift in power, but a shift in creativity. Creativity had ridden the era of the Church as far as it could be ridden. The institution of the Church, at first providing an encouraging environment or at the least a relatively safe one for which people could better their lives, ended up becoming not the solution to a problem but the problem itself. Humankind was taking the strides forward that the Church was attempting to hinder. But creativity is like a continuous increase of rushing water, relentlessly finding its way. This is the nature of human advancement. For a certain period of significant progress, the order of the Church successfully held the rush, harnessed its power, even gave it a place to rise and made use of it. It can be thought of as a reservoir, but in the case of human creativity, it's a reservoir that continues to rise. You can build a dam and you can keep building it higher, but in the end, the water is going to find a way over the dam, around the dam, or through the dam. The problem is not the water. Water is a natural phenomenon. The problem is the dam. And when the dam ultimately breaks down, the options are limited. One either goes along with the current or sticks with the ill-fated dam.

With creativity, those who successfully harness the new direction of the current will be those who reap its power. For the monarchs, they sensed the new direction. They knew things weren't working as before. The failed Crusades, the Black Death, the Protestant Reformation, new economic thinking, and new scientific advancements in direct opposition to Church dogma (Galileo, picking up on the scientific ideas of Copernicus and adding some of his own, was found guilty of heresy by the Inquisition in 1633 and put under house arrest where he would die eleven years later) – it all added up to an environment that made Europe ripe for change. The water was rising. The only remaining question was this: Where would the current lead? Harnessing its power meant getting out in front of it, which is exactly what the monarchs were capable of doing.

Throughout history, this sequence – born of humankind's innate need to continuously create – has repeated itself regularly:

World Order

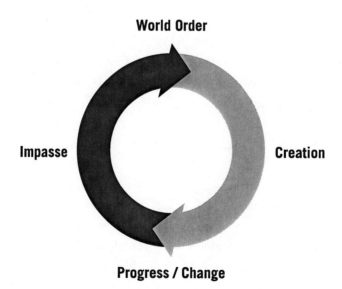

Impasse

Creation

Progress / Change

It's important to note that the geopolitical structure of the world at any given time – the world order – is never the prevailing power. Those in power gain their power *from* the structure, but are not the structure itself. They work, to their own benefit, within the confines of the order. During the order of Absolutism, for instance, world power shifted, in turns, among the monarchs of France and Spain and England and Portugal and the Dutch Republic. It was not, that is to say, the monarchs, but the monarchs *collectively* that represented the era's world order. Power comes and goes, but the structure remains in place (until the next order). In time, the monarchs' collective power receded, not because they were failing in and of themselves, or even governing themselves much differently than they had at the beginning of the order. Their power receded because the *structure* began to fail. And with it, the creative expression of humankind itself began to ebb. But not for long. Never for long. Creativity continues, always seeking its own level, finding it eventually in the next order, and creating wealth and power along the way for custodians of the new structure who have the foresight to follow where humankind's creativity is leading.

If human creativity is the force behind history's great periods of progress, it's worthwhile to consider just how creativity becomes translated into such advancement. What defines an era of monumental productivity? Conversely, what is it, then, that must go missing when the era begins its downswing? This question obviously doesn't lack import. The economic decline of the Age of Discovery and the eras of the First and Second Industrial Revolution resulted in nothing less than global war. When creativity becomes impeded, what exactly are the ramifications on the wellbeing of the world? What are the symptoms of its degradation?

CHAPTER FOUR

Value Creation

*We can have democracy in this country, or we can have
great wealth concentrated in the hands of a few,
but we can't have both.*
JUSTICE LOUIS D. BRANDEIS

Which of humankind's creations was the most significant,
the one creating the most value? Which has moved the species
forward the most? Was it the harnessing of fire? The wheel?
Or was it written language, the printing press, the steam
engine, the light bulb, penicillin, or the computer? Most certainly, there's no single valid answer. But surely one of the
more fascinating stories of advancement has to be the account
of humankind's development of food production. After all,
without readily accessible food, there would be no humans,
at least not in the numbers that populate the earth today.

Less than three centuries ago, more than three-quarters
of the world's working population were involved in agriculture
and still there was not enough food to consistently go around.
Famine, war, and plague, many times related, continually

limited the world's population, which could never exceed the agricultural infrastructure supporting it. But with advances from the British Agricultural Revolution in the eighteenth century, the Industrial Revolution of the nineteenth century, and countless innovations that followed, the world's population was able to grow from around 700 million in the mid-1700s to more than seven *billion* today. And overall, less than one-third of the world's workers today are involved in agriculture, less than 5% in Europe and North America. The services sector now employs more workers worldwide than the agriculture sector. The world's farmlands yield significantly more food now per acre, with better crops, in a shorter time, and with less labor and energy. The story of humankind's advancement in food production represents a revolution in efficiency. And that revolution has allowed for the creation of enormous value.

What is value creation? Not the intangible value of, say, gold or diamonds, but the value related to productivity and creation? For something to be substantively valuable, it needs to save us time, use less space than we're using, or make more efficient use of what we have. Getting more mileage out of the gas you put into your car is productive. Taking the empty corner of the lot where a house sits and building an apartment to rent for extra income is productive. Bringing oil to the surface where it's worth something is productive. Moreover, it's not a zero sum game. If it's productive, it's not taking from some other productive enterprise in an equivalent amount. It's the creation of something new, something that wasn't there before. This kind of productivity is what's witnessed during long periods of economic expansion.

With each economic boom that has occurred over the last five centuries (Age of Discovery, Industrial Revolution, Second Industrial Revolution, and Space-Digital Age), this is precisely what happened. Those global economies were driven by the new order of things, flush with new technology and capital investment, unbridled by past debt and marked by optimism about the future. Economically speaking, these were exceptional and extraordinary periods where everything came together at once – opportunities expanded, production and consumption escalated, employment rose, and incomes grew. Value and wealth were created.

Periods of real wealth creation are marked by very high productivity – significant increases in the utilization of time, space, or matter. The efficiency created by the productivity naturally creates excess capacity. It creates "slack." Finding a faster way to do something leaves us with more time on our hands, for example. But the benefit of productivity is only realized if the slack can be redeployed elsewhere. If an apartment is built onto a lot but the apartment sits vacant, that's not very productive. What's really been created?

Or let's say a factory replaces its workers with a robotic assembly line. The factory may be more productive, using fewer inputs of capital and labor to produce more efficient outputs, and the factory may see its profits soar. But what happens to the displaced factory workers? If they don't find new employment at a similar or improved pay scale, was the factory's productivity additive to the economy as a whole? If this isolated example were to occur throughout an entire economy, it would lead to an unsustainable situation.

In boom times, we don't notice the slack because it gets redeployed. But we often don't notice it in other times, either, mainly because there are ways in which idle slack can become obscured. By debt, for instance. In the robotic assembly line example, suppose the displaced workers, wanting to keep up the same standard of living they had prior to being laid off, decide to borrow money against hoped-for future income. Maybe they start charging everything to their credit cards. From the outside looking in, it still appears as though everyone's being productive. The robotic assembly line is producing goods and the laid-off workers are buying them. But of course what's not being produced is wealth. In this little microcosm, the economy is being financed by debt, which must eventually be paid. It's not supporting itself, in other words.

It's fair to characterize each of the boom times of the last five centuries like so: very high productivity and wealth creation covered most of society, the wealth creation was not a zero-sum game across all the various sectors, slack was created but then redeployed because of plentiful opportunity, the overall standard of living rose, capital investment opportunities were competing for money and not the other way around where money competes for opportunity, and there were no shortages of the required natural resources. It is also safe to say that these boom times lasted only between thirty to fifty years or a couple of generations.

Conversely, when the global economy is not in a boom time, all of the characteristics above become their opposites. This is what happens to whole economies at the end of boom times. Widespread wealth creation starts to wane. There is not enough new opportunity for displaced slack, consumptive debt grows, capital investment diminishes, and economic disparity starts to trend larger.

It is also important to note that never – never – have boom times come back to back.

So why do boom times end? In large part, it's a natural byproduct of the technological-productive life cycle. During the boom, new technologies are widely implemented and distributed. Significant capital investment is made and there is an expected life over which that investment remains in place. A return must be made on it. With a long-term commitment now positioned for this technology, new directions and potential new technologies go by the wayside. Think of the fledgling airplane industry prior to the world wars. The technology came into existence, but capital formation was hardly anywhere to be found. Too much investment money had been tied up in the railroads and nobody was going to abandon them. It was only during the wars, particularly World War II, that money would go into the new technology of flight, and it was money spent by governments to exploit the technology not for monetary gain, but for use in combat. Plus, there's something of human nature at work. We have a tendency to want to rest on our laurels, riding whatever the dominant technology is as far as we can. We become complacent with the familiar and happy with the status quo. Staying with the familiar seems easier and less painful than change.

And so, without some impetus (like war) to focus direction on the application of new technologies, the technologies of the day will be allowed to run their course. But over the life of the investment, the rate of return will begin to diminish as the market becomes saturated. At this point, producers fulfill mostly for obsolescence and profits start to stagnate unless a lower cost of capital can be found. Debt becomes the solution. For a while. But of course, more and more debt ultimately becomes the problem. When a boom time produces a large amount of technologies with widespread growth and long-term capital commitments (first with equity and then with debt), all of these processes tend to start and "expire" at around the same time. The boom ends and a period of slower wealth creation and stagnation ensues.

The problem is that we never really see the tipping point, the point at which financing a business slow-down becomes economically dangerous. It's human nature to assume that better times are ahead if we can just get through the rough patch. And sometimes those better times are ahead. But sometimes they're not. We see this all the time on an individual basis. A person works his or her whole adult life and lives the American dream and builds a good life. But then something happens in mid-life. Maybe a layoff or illness or divorce. Maybe the person is replaced by someone who's less experienced but willing to work more cheaply. Suddenly the person's standard of living is threatened. The house payment is at risk, the annual trip to Europe becomes a question mark. But with confidence in the future, the standard of living gets maintained. By a home equity loan, perhaps. Or credit card debt. Or by dipping into the retirement account. This happens to people and it happens at an institutional level as well. By all outward appearances, things seem the same as they were. But of course they're not. If the person can't find a new opportunity to support the established standard of living, then the tipping point has already been passed. Negative savings or debt will only make the situation more precarious. Slack is not being redeployed, but it appears so, being paid for with value creation that has already come (savings) or has yet to come (debt). Either way, it's not current value creation, and it's not sustainable. So long as the slack is not redeployed, it's kicking the can down the road, and of course the farther the can gets kicked, the worse the ultimate reconciliation will be. When entire economies kick the can down the road, the reconciliation can be disastrous.

So when looking at the world's economy, how can we tell where we are in this cycle? How can we tell if we're in a period of real expansion where wealth is being created or a period of expansion by debt? Economists like to measure expansion by using Gross Domestic Product. GDP can be measured by how much the country's population is spending, or by how much the country's population is earning. Over time, these two numbers should theoretically be the same. If somebody is spending, somebody else is earning. It's axiomatic.

GDP doesn't necessarily tell us much about productivity or wealth creation, though. A country's GDP can rise due to its increase in collective debt. If that apartment is built, expenditures for the owner increase and the contractor's income increases as well. What's not seen is the fact that the contractor has been paid with a loan from a bank. This doesn't really matter in good times. Debt gets rolled over and the absolute level of the country's debt remains relatively constant or modestly expands. One person might take out a loan while another person pays his loan off. GDP becomes a useful tool, then, because the debt isn't a significant factor. In periods where real productivity or real wealth creation is slowing, GDP becomes less useful, if not altogether unreliable as a qualitative measure for the economy. When wealth creation or productivity slows, naturally a drop in income and GDP will follow. However, if there is a rapid rise in debt and the proceeds from the debt are used to support consumptive spending levels – previously supported by current wealth creation – then GDP won't drop and the health of the economy will be distorted.

GDP statistics rise with the population, too. More people mean more demand for goods and services. But this type of increase doesn't equate to relative growth *per person*. Nobody notices it, in other words, on an individual basis. Suppose the Federal Reserve announces or projects after-inflation GDP growth at 1% per year and the population also grows by 1%. Then the economy *is* expanding, but only on an absolute basis. For instance, the United States population has been growing recently by roughly three million people per year. GDP has risen as well. But, adjusted for population growth and inflation, the GDP per capita was the same in 2013 as it was five years earlier in 2008. (Beginning in 2008 there was a decline that bottomed out in 2010. Finally, in 2013, the 2008 level was regained.) Therefore, a more relevant measure when evaluating wealth creation might be "real" GDP per capita. This essentially answers the question of what GDP means for the typical person. It's a standard-of-living gauge, essentially.

But this too has its inherent limitations. GDP per capita may not disclose a widening gap of financial inequality.

Instead of GDP, with its emphasis on spending and income, what we really need to focus on is a way to accurately measure debt. How much of an economy is expanding through real wealth creation versus how much of it is expanding through debt, especially consumer debt? This is the pertinent question. Unfortunately, it's not an easy task to get a handle on the amount of an economy's debt. We can get some idea by considering the aggregate amount of bank loans taken out, but there exists an entire system of non-bank financial intermediaries (hedge funds, private equity funds, finance companies, etc.) that economists like to refer to as the shadow banking system. It's virtually impossible to know how much debt is being funded by these largely unregulated entities.

Shadow banking was a huge factor in the subprime crisis, though it's not fair to paint the shadow banking system as the villain. Shadow banking serves a legitimate purpose and it can be additive to a prosperous economy. Its existence is not the issue. Rather, it's the lack of available information from the system that's problematic. The opaqueness of the shadow banking system adds to the dilemma of determining exactly where an economy may be in the grand cycle of wealth creation.

In addition to the non-bank intermediaries of the shadow banking system, there are a slew of "off balance sheet" financial instruments and other commitments (credit derivatives) that represent future obligations that are almost impossible to measure. These are more common than you might think. You might be tied to an obligation of this sort even now. Take for example your mobile device purchase contract. Most cell phone users sign up for at least an annual use commitment when they acquire their phone. Sure, you can get out of the contract, but at what price? At a minimum, the termination charge could be considered the future obligation. Or maybe you stick with the contract and your future obligation is the actual amount of committed monthly payments. People may scoff at the inconsequential nature of these types of consumer obligations, but when all the different goods and services purchased under some form of quasi-commitment are added up, it's astonishing how little of an economy's true disposable or discretionary income remains.

Recognizing the difficulties of measuring just where the economy is, economists like to use something called multifactor productivity (MFP). High productivity could be a sign of real wealth creation. MFP measures the change in the economy's output as a factor of certain inputs, like labor and capital. Theoretically, if there's a lot of output, but relatively little input, it indicates strong productivity. We're getting more bang for the buck, and that additional bang can only be explained by greater efficiency – in other words, a saving somewhere along the line of space, time, or matter. But MFP can be tricky. It's extremely difficult to gather all the necessary data to make an accurate measurement, and therefore MFP becomes subject to a large sampling error. Moreover, the amount of actual capital input is difficult to measure. But most importantly, the MFP measurement gives us only a dated sense of productivity, telling us nothing about the future, or even where we are at this moment, since the data is naturally historical. Economists sometimes like to make projections based on where we've recently been, but the problem with trying to say what the next six months will look like based on the last six months should be obvious. One is reminded of the standard disclaimer for all investments: *Past performance is not indicative of future results.*

Some people like to point to specific technological advances as confirmation of productivity. This brings us back to the concept that technological innovation needs to be utilized in a productive way in order for us to claim some value in that productivity. The vacant apartment means an unproductive innovation. Along those lines, it's worth considering our more recent digital innovations. We've made great strides, for example, in the way we listen to music. We've gone from vinyl to cassette to MP3s to listening to music on our smart phones, which can now hold thousands of songs. Nobody can argue that this is not amazing. It borders on the miraculous. Yet, how productive is it? How have we created or saved time, space, or matter? One needs to be careful when one considers the latest upgrades and enhancements as representative of an economy in a wealth-creating upswing. It may be the case, it may not be. How does the latest advance save time, space, or matter? And what are we doing with the savings? How are we taking up the slack? Those are the important questions.

In the end analysis, it must be admitted that sometimes we just can't see where we are economically in any given time period while that time period is unfolding. Only later can we look back and see what was happening. But though it's not very scientific, there are moments when we can at least *sense* a period of contraction while we're in it, even if we can't quantifiably prove it. In their daily lives, most people eschew the fancy calculations of the economists in favor of their own experiences. Ask someone how he thinks the economy is doing and he'll consider his own bank account. He'll think of his own level of debt – his credit cards, his mortgage, and his monthly obligations. He might think of his neighbors, too, or his family members. People talk. We get a sense of how things are anecdotally. Economists talk about an upswing in the economy, but the guy who's just gotten laid off from his manufacturing job in Detroit isn't going to be convinced, nor is the single mom who's barely eking out a living as a waitress in the service sector. Maybe it's not easy to quantify, but this sense that we have is not to be underestimated. Often, too, we can see palpable evidence of economically questionable times in the level of general dissatisfaction in a population of people, frequently finding its source in financial inequality, a certain hallmark of a reduction in wealth creation, leading to an imbalance in the ownership of wealth.

History shows that when booms go bust, and the busts get bad enough, the consequences can be catastrophic. This is especially true with the world's greatest periods of value creation: the Age of Discovery, the First Industrial Revolution, and the Second Industrial Revolution (history has yet to reveal the consequences that will follow the Space-Digital Age). At the ends of these periods, the downward spiral was significant enough to ultimately force nothing less than a new world order as a means of moving humankind forward once again from where it stalled. And the new order always came in on war – global in its reach.

CHAPTER FIVE

The Widening Gap

*An imbalance between rich and poor is the oldest
and most fatal ailment of all republics.*
PLUTARCH, GREEK PHILOSOPHER (C. 46-120 A.D.)

One of the most important – and dangerous – symptoms of an economy lacking wealth creation, opportunity, and productivity, is severe economic inequality. At the end of the major productivity cycles, as the world moved closer to the end of the existing global order, one can find significant disparity between the "haves" and the "have-nots." English and French aristocracy prior to the American Revolution, Southern plantation owners and the European nobility prior to the wars of the mid-1800s, and prosperous industrialists prior to the Great Depression (think Rockefeller and Carnegie), were the haves during those critical times of stressed economies and global angst. During these times, the gap between the wealthy class and the rest of the world's population was generally at its widest.

It's important to recognize how this disparity happens.

As the world order loses effectiveness in producing wealth and opportunity, those reaping any rewards from the economy become fewer and fewer. It becomes a game of last man standing. And the haves during these particular zero-sum periods are the ones who have already gained the most under the current structure of the world. They continue to maintain power and control, so long as something can be wrung out of the dwindling economy. Eventually, of course, the structure will have to change and a new order will be required. But until then, those who have will continue to take at the expense of those who do not have. And the inequality will continue to grow.

Inequality can be considered as income inequality or wealth inequality. As one might assume, income inequality is the disparity between individuals or groups with respect to the flow of money – salaries, wages, or retirement income, for instance. Wealth inequality is the disparity in what is owned – homes and investments and businesses and savings accounts and other assets. Wealth inequality is often a better measure of the difference between the haves and have-nots because income inequality doesn't always tell the whole story. In the long run, a person's level of financial well-being is more a factor of what he owns than what he earns. But wealth disparity isn't always noticed. Especially in good times, when people's incomes are generally rising, it matters little to them that somebody might own more than they do. Or at least they can tolerate the difference. It's when incomes start to decrease that people begin to notice the gap in wealth. Either way, we can combine the concepts for the sake of simplicity and talk in terms of *financial* inequality.

Financial inequality can occur within a society, and it can occur between societies. The French Revolution is a decent example of the former, while 1930s Germany relative to the rest of Europe serves as a good example of the latter, although

Germany had significant imbalances within their society as well. We might also look to today's Middle East to see both at the same time – inequality within the Arab nations (to a degree leading to uprisings; i.e., the Arab Spring), as well as huge disparities between some Middle Eastern nations such as Yemen and Syria versus others such as Saudi Arabia, Qatar, and United Arab Emirates. However it occurs, financial inequality at the end of an order is always widespread, a general condition that is observable throughout the world.

It must be said that it's not an easy task to demonstrate through historical statistics the financial inequality that existed towards the ends of our world orders. Only in relatively recently times has adequate data on financial inequality been collected and maintained. And anyway, statistics can be notoriously easy to manipulate to any given argument's advantage. But actions often speak louder than statistics and it's in the actions of the masses during these times that we can see the disparity that created the world's tension which, in each case, continued to build until the respective conflict became a foregone conclusion.

We've pointed to the French Revolution as an example. Something similar was brewing in England around the same time. The economies of both countries were in shambles. Wealth creation had waned and debt had soared. The resulting Credit Crisis of 1772 had created panic. The standard of living was in rapid decline. And it was, of course, much worse for the peasant class than for the nobility. King George III felt pressured to alleviate the concerns of his restless population and so, without the means by which to create new wealth, he sought the wealth of the American colonists through taxation and burdensome trade policies. As for the colonists, financial inequality within their society was much less of a problem. The colonies were much more egalitarian than Great Britain. Yes, there were wealthy landowners, but the economic load placed on the colonies by the King cut across all classes and when the relatively prosperous (now economically threatened) Founding Fathers headed towards war, the poor jumped on board with them. Ultimately, it was the financial inequality in Europe that set in motion the chain of events that would launch both the revolution in America and the overthrow of the French king.

By the mid-nineteenth century, the effects of the Industrial Revolution had slowed and financial inequality again reached extreme levels, this time in the U.S. as well. There were wealthy industrialists in the north and wealthy plantation owners in the south, but there were starving workers and slaves, respectively, too; not that anyone would have bothered including slaves in any income or employment analysis of the time. But their presence was a significant factor on the downward pressure of wages, a fact that did not go unnoticed by northern laborers who watched the South come through the Panic of 1857 enviably untouched.

But the financial inequality, coming at the end of the Industrial Revolution's worldwide productivity boom, was a significant phenomenon experienced beyond the borders of just the U.S. The year 1848 became known in Europe as the "Year of Revolution" or the "Spring of Nations" (bringing to mind today's recent Arab Spring). The uprisings started in France and spread to most of the continent, even jumping across the world to Latin America. No less than fifty countries experienced some level of revolution and tens of thousands were killed. To this day the revolts collectively represent the most extensive revolutionary movement in European history. The participants were as varied and many as the reasons, but there was one rather large common denominator and that was the issue of class. The working classes, the peasants, and the urban poor were united in their disaffection, the working classes being the most disaffected since they were the ones previously most satisfied when the economic effect of the Industrial Revolution was in its prime.

All around the world, tradesmen and general laborers had either been displaced by the technology of the Industrial Revolution or had lost their standing, becoming overworked and underpaid factory employees in the crowded cities. Former agricultural workers had also moved to the cities to find work in the factories. With the dissatisfaction of the working class adding to the already existing plights of the peasants and serfs, the conditions were ripe for unrest once the inevitable downturn in productivity came. The revolutionaries were also emboldened by new ideas of nationalism and socialism and communism. Today, most connect Marx with Stalin and the Russian Revolution of 1917. But it was in February of 1848 in London that Karl Marx published *The Communist Manifesto*. Although written in German, the political manuscript was so controversial and its acclaim so widespread throughout France, Britain, Germany, and the rest of Europe, that Marx was arrested or threatened with arrest all over the continent for years to come. Government leaders and those in the wealthy class castigated Marx for the spark that lit the tinderbox of 1848. The legacy of *The Communist Manifesto* cannot be denied, even today, but in 1848 it was especially significant. Class struggle was in the world's spotlight. And it was financial inequality that had pushed it onto the stage.

The lower classes' disaffection in Europe at the time might even be better evidenced by the enormous numbers of people leaving their homelands for the perceived opportunities in America. In the 1840s, U.S. immigration tripled from the decade before. But poor Irish, German, British, and French immigrants expanded the American lower class, further increasing the pressures of U.S. financial inequality and adding to the turbulence of the pre-Civil War nation.

In the next century, it was the financial inequality following the Second Industrial Revolution, best reflected by the Great Depression. The world's greatest economic catastrophe to date spawned a restless dissatisfaction of the deprived that turned almost mythic in proportion: "What do you want us to do?" laments a character in Steinbeck's emblematic *Grapes of Wrath*. "We can't take less share of the crop – we're half starved now. The kids are hungry all the time. We got no clothes, torn an' ragged. If all the neighbors weren't the same, we'd be ashamed to go to meeting." Twenty-five percent unemployment (up to 33% elsewhere in the world) created bread lines and soup lines and a class of abject poverty where a comfortable middle class used to exist.

Frustration was evident with the rise of strikes and riots. A hunger march of unemployed auto workers in 1932 Detroit turned into a violent melee in which five of the marchers were shot and killed by police. In the spring and summer of that year, thousands of mostly out-of-work veterans of World War I descended on Washington D.C. to claim bonuses owed them for their service. They had received "service certificates" that could not be redeemed until 1945. Although the certificates were accruing interest, the veterans needed the money then and there. They camped in one of the nearby "Hoovervilles" (shanty towns built by the homeless and mockingly named after then-President Herbert Hoover) and marched down Pennsylvania Avenue. Hoover ordered the Army to remove them from their camp and the 12th Infantry Regiment, led by General Douglas MacArthur, and the 3rd Cavalry Regiment, complete with six tanks and commanded by Major George Patton, rushed the camp, lobbing teargas and burning the veterans' tents. It was a bizarre incident, and the over-the-top order by Hoover to send the Army after Army veterans was the final nail in his political coffin. For the sitting president, already perceived as being out of touch with the ordinary suffering citizen and being too sympathetic to big business and big banks, the Bonus Army revolt, as it came to be called, only made matters worse. Hoover's train and motorcades were routinely pelted with eggs during his 1932 campaign trail for re-election, a contest he lost in a landslide to Franklin Delano Roosevelt.

In his 1951 memoir *Beckoning Frontiers*, Marriner Eccles, the former Chairman of the Federal Reserve who served during the Great Depression era, described the then-financial inequality as a "giant suction pump" drawing into the hands of the few an increasing amount of the produced wealth. Eccles observed, "In consequence, as in a poker game where the chips were concentrated in fewer and fewer hands, the other fellows could stay in the game only by borrowing. When their credit ran out, the game stopped." Eccles and the Federal Reserve's actions during the Depression and World War II were directly aimed at redistributing wealth away from the suction pump. Of course, this caused great consternation amongst the wealthy. Many of the redistribution policies were only possible under the backdrop of drastic measures implemented for survival during the war. In 1942, in some of the gloomiest days following the attack on Pearl Harbor and other early U.S. setbacks in the Pacific war against the Japanese, Congress, at the insistence of FDR, Eccles, and other New Deal reformers, passed an income tax of 94% on incomes over $200,000 ($2.8 million in today's dollars). FDR was actually pushing for a significantly lower ceiling of $50,000 ($700,000 today). The extreme tax rate on the higher brackets remained in effect for decades, long after the war, repealed eventually when the top 1% of Americans earned only 10% of the country's income. World War II had allowed for the toppling of the status quo.

Posterity will remember, and for great reason, the ideological and military crusades of these three periods – liberty and the American and French Revolutions, slavery and the U.S. Civil War, and fascism and World War II. These crusades unquestionably achieved major milestones in the ascent of humankind. But the consideration of any of those epic struggles is incomplete if, in the final analysis, the context of financial inequality is ignored.

Today, of course, financial inequality is back in the spotlight. There are haves and have-nots, within and across the world's societies. The nations that have are essentially the U.S., Japan, Germany, the United Kingdom, France, Australia, and Canada. These seven countries, representing 13% of the world's population, collectively receive 45% of the world's income and control more than half of the world's wealth. North America and Europe seems to be where most of the wealth is concentrated (along with a select few Middle Eastern countries like Qatar or UAE), while the impoverished continue to be countries in Africa and South Asia. Overall, a recent study by the World Institute for Development Economics Research at United Nations University found that, collectively, the world's wealthiest 1% of individuals own 40% of the world's assets. The richest 10% own a whopping 85% of the world's assets.

In the United States, financial inequality seems to be growing. During the recent Great Recession, median household wealth fell for the top 1% by 11.1%, but for the other 99%, wealth dropped by over 36%. And the recovery has followed the same uneven course. Income inequality continues to be at an extreme level for the country; today, the U.S. ranks in the bottom third of all the world's countries based on income distribution. The top 1% of the American population receives over 20% of its income, nearly matching the levels established during the Depression era.

As for wealth disparity, note the graph below. Economists Emmanuel Saez and Gabriel Zucman ("Wealth Inequality in the United States since 1913: Evidence from Capitalized Income Tax Data," revised and resubmitted *Quarterly Journal of Economics,* August 2015) have calculated that today, over 20% of U.S. wealth is held by 0.1% of the population – approximately 160,000 families out of an estimated one-hundred million. To find an historically similar level, one needs to go back to 1928 – the eve of the Great Depression.

Top 0.1% Wealth Share in the United States: 1913-2012

As can be seen, the latest inequality had its beginnings back in the early 1980s. But the economy was growing, and it wasn't necessarily noticed by most people. And if it was, there were ways to deal with it, ways to compensate. Families with a single-wage earner (typically the male) became dual-income families. Thirty years later, the stay-at-home mom has become a rarity. But what happens when even a second income is insufficient? Then people seek other alternatives in order to compensate – borrowing, for example, with home equity loans and lines of credit. Naturally, without an increase in income (or an increase in the value of the home), this is hardly sustainable. Where is the viable alternative for the family having trouble making ends meet today? The options have become exhausted and financial inequality is as obvious as an open wound. The "American Dream" is becoming a distant memory.

As in prior periods, the data are hardly necessary. People directly experience the inequality in job loss and lack of opportunity. The latter is what becomes especially problematic. There will always be inequality so long as there are varying degrees of skills and talents. People are not inherently equal in their aptitudes, and forcing an equal outcome (say, through wealth distribution) for non-equivalent proficiencies chafes against human nature (and is bad economics to boot). But a very American idea is that people ought to be equal in their potentialities. We all ought to have the same level of opportunity available to us, relative to our strengths. The loss of this idea can be dangerous to a democracy. If a certain percentage of a country's population comes to believe that they are living in a system in which opportunity is only for "other" people, then resentment and divisiveness fester. If that percentage happens to be relatively young – think of those in their twenties and thirties who have grown up witnessing nothing else but the increasing divide between the haves and have-nots since the early '80s – then you have the potential for an especially explosive situation.

It is when opportunity is squelched that the inequality gap is most keenly felt, first because it's more noticeable in a first-hand kind of way (ask someone who's just been displaced and rendered jobless), and second because it is indeed at these times of low opportunity that the gap demonstrably widens. The haves continue to own the wherewithal and the opportunities that go with it.

But why is the gap widening? How did this state of affairs come about? There may be a myriad of reasons. Globalization is a culprit often pointed to. Low-wage workers in Asia, for example, have displaced low-skilled American workers in the manufacturing fields. The increase in global competition from the emergence of the so-called BRIC countries (Brazil, Russia, India, China) has cost American jobs and put downward pressure on wages.

Meanwhile, the rapid pace of technology has increased the demand for higher-educated workers, thus lowering the demand in the marketplace of employees produced by the U.S. school system, which currently ranks behind most of the industrialized countries and many of the emerging countries. This trend has led to a distinct divide between the haves of technological know-how and the have-nots of lower-skilled, blue-collar labor. Moreover, the number of lesser-educated workers has increased through higher levels of immigration since the mid-1960s. The lower class has grown, in part, due to the burgeoning population of immigrants, and that population has grown through a higher-than-national-average birthrate.

Some analysts point to soaring executive compensation as a contributing cause to today's financial inequality. By 2006, CEOs of American companies were making 400 times more than their average employees, a gap twenty times bigger than in 1965. Meanwhile, middle income pay has been stagnating, and more regressive taxation brought about by political forces has muddled the effects of free-market forces. Over the past few decades, the highest income tax rates have been reduced. So have capital gains taxes. The net effect has been rent-seeking in nature; wealth merely shifts from one set of pockets to another set of fewer pockets, with no significant contribution towards increased productivity, wealth creation, or opportunity.

And rent-seeking, aptly described by *The Economist* as "cutting yourself a bigger slice of the cake rather than making the cake bigger," often happens in far from obvious ways. We see a high-profile IPO in, say, the technology market, and we assume wealth is being created. Facebook's IPO was the biggest in history. Yet Facebook's business is driven by a finite pool of advertising revenue which is ultimately paid for by consumers. Nothing, in other words, is created. Advertising dollars shift from one venue to another and the money to finance the advertising comes from the same set of consumer pockets. Companies aren't increasing their advertising budgets to accommodate the relatively new venue of the Internet. Instead, they're pulling those dollars from other venues. The Internet is forcing advertising dollars to move down an ever-narrowing stream. Whereas the advertising industry was once composed of multiple media outlets – television, radio, print, etc. – employing millions of people, now it's centered more and more on a single outlet (the online world) that supports far fewer people. This is a classic example of rent-seeking that generally goes unnoticed. What's worse, in rent-seeking, the shift is typically uphill. The less well-off continue to lose ground to the wealthier, and financial inequality grows.

Inequality has also grown in part because we are less unionized these days. Organized advocacy for workers has declined and jobs are shipped overseas with little or no political impediments. There are valid economic arguments against unionized labor, especially when labor is less specialized and capable of being exported to lower cost jurisdictions. But if the only thing considered is the input cost of labor, the big picture gets missed. The full cost to a society – when the result is financial inequality – is greater than it might appear.

The story of financial inequality cannot be told with unemployment statistics. When jobs are lost, we don't always notice it right away. Initially, a job lost is often replaced by another; a middle manager gets laid off, so he takes a position elsewhere. Looking strictly at unemployment numbers, there's no difference. What's not seen, however, is that the former middle manager has taken a pay cut to remain employed. He was earning, say, $80,000 in his mid-to upper-level position; now he's working the counter at Subway. But of course, what he's really lost can't be quantitatively measured. In his previous position, he had the potential to be far more *productive*. He's lost that opportunity. It's a loss for the economy as well.

If the effect on equality caused by job loss is not noticed at first, neither is the difference in consumption. Our new Subway employee had become accustomed to a certain lifestyle that he's intent on maintaining – through savings that he's accumulated over the years or even by way of the equity in his home. In the aggregate, an economy that is shifting its job base clicks along like business as usual, until the collective savings begins to run out or the home equity loans begin to pile up beyond what is sustainable. At this point, we suddenly begin to notice that income has dropped and debt has risen. Worse, the lower class has now become a lot larger and the gap between it and the wealthy has widened significantly. What really goes missing in an economy such as this is the middle class itself. Those who comprise it find themselves shifted to the lower half of the economic spectrum. In the meantime, the middle class rises where the jobs have moved. The diminishing American middle class has moved to the BRIC countries.

The underlying problem is that when aggregate wealth creation begins to flatline, an unfortunate zero-sum game unfolds. With no new productivity from which to sustain oneself, one takes from what is already in existence. This is the rent-seeking shifting of wealth, the shift typically towards those most capable of taking it – the already wealthy. Unable to tap into existing wealth, the rest of the population borrows against future (hoped-for) wealth, thus driving themselves further into debt and further away from the wealth holders. The gap widens and ultimately it will widen on a global level where resentment festers and class warfare ensues.

Rent-seeking activity in an economy, as opposed to real wealth creation, is the number one culprit that drives a society's financial inequality higher.

Of course governments will do what they can to try to alleviate significant financial inequality. More progressive taxation is frequently the first recourse, taking from the wealthier in an effort to more "fairly" redistribute the country's wealth. But without increased productivity and opportunity, this serves only to delay the inevitable. It's understandable, of course, that policymakers would yield to the cries from their constituency to "do something." Inaction breeds contempt from the disaffected and ultimately, history shows, revolt. Wealth distribution, on the other hand, unsurprisingly breeds contempt from those with the wealth. Either way, conflict becomes unavoidable. And either way, there's really no long-term difference a policymaker can create. Shifting of wealth without an increase in opportunity and total wealth creation merely kicks the can down the road.

Sometimes the attention goes towards education. There's a push to bring the lower class back to middle-class status by providing them the tools to better compete in a world of new technology. And yet simply making everyone computer engineers does nothing in and of itself to increase productivity. Without growth fueled by productivity, you simply have a lot of computer engineers with no place to go. Perhaps in the aggregate you can bring certain efficiencies to bear, but to what end? Efficiencies often create the displacement of workers. This isn't a problem in a growing economy; the workers are picked up elsewhere. But in a sliding economy, the displacement equates to job loss. Investment and innovation in and of themselves do not represent productivity. The slack that's created by increased efficiency has to be taken up somewhere else in the economy. If opportunities aren't created – that is to say if wealth isn't created – you can't call it productivity.

With competition from foreign job markets displacing workers through cheaper labor, governments often attempt to stop companies from moving their operations out of the country by creating tax incentives or other breaks designed to make companies stay put and hire locally. It's more rent-seeking and on a global basis. At best, the strategy might slow the trend of migrating jobs. And without a growing global economy, it's not a long-term global solution. It provides an advantage for one country's workers to the detriment of another country's workers. The unintended consequence is more financial inequality.

Another source of unintended consequences is the level of complexity that the government often introduces in its cumbersome attempts to help. As a means by which to shift the flow of money, the tax code gets revised, incentivizing and-or de-incentivizing certain behaviors. Those with the wherewithal – the wealthy – quickly discover the best ways in which to use the new code to their advantage. Complexities in healthcare administration, environmental legislation, business formation – it all helps to create an environment best suited to the people with the best attorneys at their disposal. Nancy Pelosi, Minority Leader of the U.S. House of Representatives, famously remarked in regards to the Affordable Care Act ("Obamacare"), "We have to pass the bill so you can find out what's in it." Regulations and policies designed to boost the little guy often have the opposite effect by raising the barrier of entry, making it more difficult to enter the market of new opportunities.

There's been a significant amount of study undertaken

on the effects of wealth inequality and redistribution, and – interestingly – the positive longer-term effects on economic growth when wealth inequality has gotten worse. China is a recent example. Prior to its remarkable growth since the turn of the millennium, China had a severe shortage of capital and savings. Their solution was to redistribute wealth, but *away* from the households who didn't have much to begin with and *towards* the GDP producers. Effectively, in the shorter term, they were squeezing more water from a rock that had very little to begin with. But in so doing, China was able to create an export-driven economy, thereby bringing longer term growth and even more (foreign) capital to the Chinese economy. Naturally, there was short-term societal pain (and dissent – recall Tiananmen Square), but it was controlled by China's totalitarian regime. But China's solution was unique to their society and their type of government. Western capitalistic nations have attempted to solve financial inequality more democratically.

This is where Marx got it wrong. Marx's contention was that every capitalist society would inevitably fail due to its tendency towards an ever-increasing concentration of wealth. Once a society reached some undefined level of inequality, revolution would follow. But when Marx was writing his thesis, he wasn't considering the democracies of today. Economists like John Maynard Keynes, arguing against Marx, maintained that democracies respond politically (even in war, e.g., the World War II tax hike) through wealth redistribution rather than revolt and that the political response would have a long-term effect (intentionally or unintentionally) of saving the wealthy class and private capital ownership, thereby guaranteeing the survivability of capitalism. Keynes noted that in democratic societies there were alternate periods of immense wealth concentration with periods of immense wealth redistribution. But what Keynes left unsaid was that the turning point between the two came by way of political measures *only* during times of great volatility when the democracies themselves were in peril, either through civil war or external threats.

Even a wealthy industrialist like Henry Ford understood the debilitating effects of wealth inequality on society. And (to no small self-interest) on his own pocketbook. Ford paid workers higher wages because he understood that only by so doing could workers afford to buy his cars. Ford was outspoken on the subject of wages, even if his fellow industrialists of the time failed to be convinced. Ford knew that higher, not lower, wages would create more consumers.

Notwithstanding any argument for or against wealth redistribution, the larger point by now should be clear: government stimulus policies in and of themselves, no matter how well intended, do nothing in the long run to effect the creation of wealth because they simply can't. The underlying problem is the dysfunction of the status quo – the end of a productivity cycle. Government policies, in fact, only serve to aggravate the problem of financial inequality by attempting to *maintain* the status quo – to hold onto an economic world that is no longer functioning.

And without new wealth creation – the primary impetus needed to narrow a financial inequality gap –, the disparities of wealth and income will be tolerated only so much. History shows this. At some point, a period of severe divisiveness occurs, either within countries, between countries, or both. When this kind of divisiveness becomes widespread, extending itself on a global level, the world starts to become a dangerous place.

CHAPTER SIX

Division

*How can you govern a country which has 246 varieties
of cheese?*
CHARLES DE GAULLE

Humanity, it is generally agreed, has never been so connected. The Internet has made the world a smaller, more
familiar place. Global trade has created whole new markets,
and products and services can be bought and sold worldwide.
On social media sites, people interact daily with others from
around the globe. News gets tweeted immediately from
Barcelona or Tokyo or Cape Town. We are closer these days,
we inhabitants of the earth.

And yet, there are seemingly countless geopolitical
hotspots around the world. The Middle East certainly doesn't
seem very connected, within the region, or to the rest of the
global society. Russia also seems a bit disconnected from
much of the world, as does North Korea. There is instability
in the South China Sea region. There is political volatility
and violence in Western and Central Africa. There is political

division throughout Europe and partisan wrangling well beyond the norm throughout the world, including the United States. Extremism seems ubiquitous and there are terror alerts everywhere.

Today's conflict and divisiveness is happening, in other words, without regard to our degree of apparent connectedness. If this seems counterintuitive, history has surprisingly shown this incongruity before. Productivity booms have always created connectivity, just as the Digital Age has created today's globalization. And yet, the booms have always ended; the world orders have always collapsed. Conflict often occurs, to put it simply, when one group begins to believe it is being disadvantaged by another group, and history's primary example of this kind of division between groups is financial inequality. And when world orders come to the ends of their useful lives, as marked by a lack of value creation leading to significant global financial inequality, connectivity is powerless to help.

Our connectedness – in trade, ideas, technology sharing, and flows of capital investment across sovereign state lines around the world – is, in its essence, no different in these respects than in the past. Just as the Internet today provides connectedness and methods of sharing for everyone with access to a computer, the Indian spice trade through ancient Roman cities during the first century was a byproduct of increased connectedness via the Silk Road. The general term "globalization" merely means the aggregate of actions worldwide that integrate civilizations, and it is far from exclusive to present day.

Moreover, our *level* of connectedness today is also not without historical precedent. Because of Internet connectedness, most people (many experts included) believe that we're more linked now than ever before. Globalization is here to stay, it is believed, and it is not imagined that any society would be able to revert to seclusion or disengagement from the rest of the world. But since the establishment of relationships between civilizations, there have always been periods of more or less "global" connectivity, the scope of which is merely relative to the status of communication and transportation technologies available at the time. Trade routes brought civilizations together as far back as two thousand years B.C. From ancient Sumer, the *Epic of Gilgamesh* (generally regarded as the world's first real work of literature) describes trade from faraway lands. Entire networks of commerce had been established. The ancient Greeks; the Roman Empire; Renaissance Europe with its use of the printing press to spread ideas in art, science, literature, technology, philosophy, and politics; the European empires of the seventeenth and eighteenth centuries – these were all very connected civilizations that, perhaps not "global" in their scope in a strict definitional sense, nonetheless enjoyed intense connectivity. Today, we are very connected according to our standards; back then, they were very connected according to theirs.

So if, in the past, civilization had already accomplished connectivity, why do we now call it "globalization" and regard the idea as something new? Primarily because it's human nature to put things into a perspective that is strongly influenced by the experience of the most recent generation. Also, humans are very good at dismissing historical patterns. We latch on to the belief that our experience is unique from that of our predecessors. We think, *this time it's different.* But by failing to view our current connectivity in an historical perspective, we run the risk of assuming conflict is a thing of the past. We conflate connectivity with unification. Therefore, we end up believing we can override natural trends, that we can yield different outcomes this time around. But what history shows is that inevitably, events occur outside of the sphere of control. Surely the Romans, for instance, could not have imagined dissolution. The very "connected" empire had been weakened internally by societal attrition but the breaking points were provided by the outside forces of barbarian invasions, disease, and environmental degradation. The result was the Dark Ages.

Today's brand of globalization is unique, however, in one important respect. Never has a world economy been so defined by it. Globalization defines today's economic structure the way mercantilism defined the order of Absolutism, for example, or laissez-faire capitalism defined the order of Self-Determination. But for now, it's important to understand that our era's connectivity is not unlike the connectivity that took place during the prior periods of great value creation in that, initially, it was a happy consequence of the boom times. During great economic upswings, everybody is more or less on the same page, going the same direction, enjoying the same collective prosperity that results from, or is enhanced by, the general convergence.

Financial inequality and divisiveness aren't necessarily absent during these periods, however. At such times, financial inequality may exist and may even grow. But the problems of divisiveness won't appear so long as the rising economic tide is lifting all boats. It's when the surge begins to recede that the byproducts of divisiveness (conflict and violence) start to reveal themselves because it is at these times that the zero-sum game begins and financial inequality is felt most keenly.

In zero-sum times, the formation of opposing factions becomes most evident, and division results to the degree that compromise between the factions becomes impossible. Not that compromise isn't sought after. Initially, it's generally regarded as being in everyone's best interest to find win-win scenarios, some sort of middle ground. By attempting compromise, each opposing party believes that concessions will make the situation still work for them. But such a state is not always available, especially after an economic boom has long ended and where the financial inequality – the loss of the vision of common benefits – is most prevalent. The economic status quo is not sustainable and no longer works for the vast majority, period. There is no way the existing conditions can remain without making inequality worse. Further economic advancement or significant increase in widespread wealth creation is actually impeded by the status quo. A pig dressed up is still a pig, no matter the amount of accessorizing by compromise attempts. The way things are *must* change and no amount of compromise will fix the lack of productivity, financial inequality, and the accompanying, underlying divisiveness.

Without dramatic change in the status quo, the trend of divisiveness becomes self-propelling, growing until one group comes to the conclusion there is simply no more to give. Compromises occur until it is reckoned that enough is enough and it is at these moments when the proverbial line gets drawn in the sand.

Divisiveness in the U.S., at least as it is revealed by political polarity, can actually be quantified. Two political scientists by the names of Keith Poole and Howard Rosenthal developed a well-respected system of measurement called the Dynamic Weighted Nominal Three Step Estimation. It's a system of comparison taking into account House and Senate roll call votes since 1789. Using Poole and Rosenthal's formula, it's apparent that in the U.S. today, we have the highest level of political divisiveness since the Civil War. This is happening in an era of what is commonly believed to be unprecedented connectedness.

How has this divisiveness come about? For one thing, it's much easier in these "connected" days of cable television and the Internet to, ironically, break into separate ideological camps. It's easier to *dis*connect. We can stick with our own kind, hang out with those who share our views, insulate our-selves from the other side. The divergent points of view fostered in our days of unity have helped us now splinter into separate interest groups and we can choose to watch either Fox News or MSNBC, depending on our political perspective, or any number of other media outlets that cater to our specific demographic. We don't tend to expand our horizons so much these days, reaching out to hear what the other guy has to say, let alone try to find ways to compromise with the other guy. Our society is less homogenous. Our shared experiences are becoming fewer and fewer. This splintering has created pockets of like-minded people who barely engage with those from other pockets. Or, apparently, recognize that they are even there: "How can the polls be neck and neck," asked Arthur Miller during the 2004 presidential election, "when I don't know one Bush supporter?"

But of course the major reason for the polarity should come as no surprise. Our polarity has increased at roughly the same pace as has the slump in wealth creation and rise in financial inequality. In addition to political camps (borne of differences on broad points of view like social issues, foreign policy, etc.), there are now the camps of the haves and the have-nots, both with a narrower focus: the economy and what to do about it. Naturally, each side has a different take and the growing antagonism is fostering increasing resentment.

One current and especially illustrative example of this festering resentment with huge economic implications is the problem of the earth's aging population. The world has never seen as aged a population as currently exists, changing the dynamics of entire countries. Non-productive segments of societies are growing larger in size and becoming more and more dependent on productive segments that are shrinking in size. Declining fertility and an increase in life-expectancy is creating, for the first time in recorded history, more people age sixty and older than people age fifteen and younger. What will this mean long-term? For one thing, it will mean a huge impact on intergenerational transfers – taxation of younger workers at unprecedented levels to pay for housing and health-care of the elderly. This is a particularly significant problem now in parts of Europe and Asia. The perceived opportunities for the young will be obfuscated by their growing financial obligations to the old. The situation will only get worse as the world's population continues to age. This will create continuing frustration for a working class already (and getting more so) frustrated by the perceived inequality of wealth. It's the have-nots being asked to pony up even more. It's more fodder for divisiveness.

How will today's divisiveness resolve itself? It's a deadly important question because once divisiveness moves beyond a certain point, it cannot, of its own accord, reverse. Reconciliation can only come about by either a major change in the status quo of the world's wealth creation, a change which is typically painful in nature (the American Civil War), or by complete dissolution of the relationship (the American Revolution), also painful. These kinds of changes are dramatic. It takes a massive counterforce to unseat the status quo. Particularly in times of great financial inequality, the leaders of the status quo are the haves. They've been the winners under the old regime. They're the ones with home court advantage and it takes a monumental (often violent) effort to unseat them.

Conflict is often deferred, of course. It's human nature to avoid discord and the consequences of it. Non-negotiable issues can remain unresolved for long periods of time. Sometimes the core issues can go unaddressed while both parties struggle with ancillary issues. Meanwhile, society's idealists often continue to hang on to the notion – in spite of evidence to the contrary – that at least some level of negotiation and compromise is still, and will always be, available. It's no coincidence that the idealists are typically on the side of the winners – the haves, the group with home court advantage. After all, their opportunity still exists; they're not experiencing the losing side of the zero-sum game that's being played out. Oftentimes, the side in power changes the subject completely, erecting a straw man issue to deflect the public's attention from the societal division taking place. (Exaggerated threats of terrorism and arguments over healthcare come to mind as U.S. examples that span a couple different administrations.) The divisiveness continues to fester underneath, of course, and in time actually becomes a symptom and measurement of a society's willingness to avoid conflict. The underlying issues become worse simply because they are allowed to go unresolved.

But stepping back for a moment, it becomes clear that there are only three possible outcomes: keep the status quo with the attendant problems and no solution; ineffectual compromise, which results in the kicking of any potential resolution down the road; or wholesale change, which has dramatic repercussions. Since the first two don't work (they don't solve the problems) the third outcome becomes inevitable.

Historically, in an attempt to shift the pain of wholesale change, to avoid internal conflict and potential dissolution, leaders have often looked for something to unify the society – a common enemy, an external threat. Tsar Nicholas II had Kaiser Wilhelm's Germany to point to, keeping the focus, at least for a short time, off the internal strife of the dying Russian economy. Hitler had the rest of Europe to point to in the 1930s, a Europe that had left Germany humiliated after World War I. Napoleon and Mussolini and Hirohito similarly found third-party villains by which to consolidate power.

Sometimes the common enemy presents itself at just the

right time and you don't even have to go looking for it. Franklin Delano Roosevelt had Hitler's Germany and Hirohito's Japan. The United States, with polarity aplenty coming out of the Great Depression, was unified in a hurry. World War II may well have been an answer to an unspoken prayer for FDR. Most likely, he knew the New Deal policies were short-term band aids for the global order that was no longer functioning. An enormous sea change was needed the world over, and it would unfold in no uncertain terms.

Naturally, leaders are reluctant to couch their motivations in economic terms. FDR couldn't speak about the economic benefits of entering into war any more than Abraham Lincoln before him. And yet both knew – both *had* to know – that regardless of the price of war, the retreat from it would lead to continued economic disparity and polarization, the likes of which would ultimately tear the country apart. Lincoln knew a civil war of some description – coming sooner or later – was a foregone conclusion. FDR averted a fatal domestic division by unifying the divided country against a common enemy. In both cases, it was the acceptance of one violent conflagration in order to prevent another violent conflagration, perhaps one even more deadly to the republic.

But neither Lincoln nor FDR could rally their fellow countrymen to arms by promising better economic conditions in a new world order or by talking in terms of a coming economic revolution that could only be avoided by war. Nobody wants to fight for the economy. It's unseemly. And so Lincoln and FDR (and every leader who ever rallied his country to war) spoke on moral and ideological grounds. This is not to say that the moral or ideological grounds – freeing the slaves, for example – weren't important or worth fighting for. But in periods of great divisiveness, periods clearly leading to ultimate dissolution of a world order, the biggest threat is economic. When world orders end, it is because value creation has slowed, a zero-sum state of affairs has begun, financial inequality has risen to precarious levels, and the world has become divided. The division can't be repaired without fixing the inequality and the inequality can't be fixed without embarking on a new wave of productivity. And new productive waves require a tear-down of the existing world structure. The Superpower order worked until it burned out, just as Nationalism before it, Self-Determination before that, Absolutism before that, and the Church order before that.

And this brings us to the ultimate consequence of divisiveness, the kind of divisiveness borne of a polarity that has rendered it unable to reverse course on its own. Where compromise has been exhausted. Where the issues have been kicked down the road as far as they can be kicked. Where the current state of affairs no longer functions and cannot be fixed. At this point, the last and only remaining opportunity to unseat the status quo is presented: war. And with it, a new trend toward unification, resulting not just from the rally to war, but also from the removal of the preexisting conditions that created the divisiveness in the first place.

If one looks carefully, one can see the very onset of war. The inevitability begins to reveal itself when the divisiveness leading to it becomes *organized*. When one observes a society's political polarity breaking the society into entrenched, uncompromising camps, the concerns of which extend beyond the day-to-day issues of government to the very nature of the government itself, one can be sure that war is imminent.

CHAPTER SEVEN

The Politics of Global War

Unless you are willing to compromise, society cannot live together. What is happening now is an increasing proportion of positions are getting beyond the point where the system can effectively hold together.
ALAN GREENSPAN

Do you think when two representatives holding diametrically opposing views get together and shake hands, the contradictions between our systems will simply melt away? What kind of a daydream is that?
NIKITA KHRUSHCHEV

When a country (or world) is in its most divisive state, the division manifests itself in extreme political volatility. Alternatives to the status quo are presented and people take sides. Movements to and away from the status quo become highly visible as the society's divisiveness becomes organized into competing factions.

History, dependably, is replete with examples. In 1614, the Estates-General met in France. This was an assembly of representatives from the three "estates" of the country: the clergy, the nobility, and the common people. Its purpose was to advise the king, but in no way could it be mistaken for a parliament or senate with any sort of political power. The king continued to have absolute say. But from time to time, he might be willing to consider the opinions of others and hence would call the Estates-General to order. To say the call was rare would be an understatement. After the 1614 assembly, the Estates-General would not be called to order for another 175 years. When it did, it was in 1789 on the eve of the French Revolution.

Even then, it wasn't necessarily King Louis XVI's idea. Two years earlier, desperate to find a solution to his country's continuing economic decline, Louis installed an Assembly of Notables. It was the Assembly of Notables which then summoned the Estates-General. The Estates-General met for several weeks but couldn't get past the very first item on the agenda – how their votes should be counted. The Third Estate, the commoners, had the larger numbers. The clergy and the nobility preferred votes to be counted by estate with each of the three sides representing a single vote, rather than counting votes by pure numbers. The king preferred this as well; the clergy and nobility were more inclined to side with the king's interests. By then, the common people were close to revolt.

In fact, revolution would come only weeks later when the Third Estate broke off from the Estates-General and formed the National Assembly. The storming of the Bastille soon followed. What had been driving the idea of revolution was (of course) the nation's precarious financial situation with its attendant financial inequality. But the economics of the situation was taking place in a larger context. This was the Age of Enlightenment. Reason and individualism were taking precedence over traditions like divine kings. And the new way of looking at the world, advanced by Rousseau and

Voltaire and other contemporary thinkers, was moving from academic philosophy to active politics, expressed most significantly in the National Assembly's *Déclaration des droits de l'homme et du citoyen* – the "Declaration of the Rights of Man and of the Citizen." The solution to the country's economic woes was no longer believed fixable *within* the system. The problem was more fundamental. The problem was the system itself.

Highly-charged political questions about the predominant system can be found in each world order change. Germany's political issues were somewhat different in the 1850s than France's in the 1770s. In 1848, Europe's "Year of Revolution," the people of the German Confederation were restless and frustrated with the ineffectiveness of the loose affiliation of the once autocratic territories, a frustration sourced (naturally) in economic breakdown. The people wanted a voice in a stronger central government, sensing that the current government was too weak to solve the region's financial difficulties. The revolt in Germany failed, but the economic need for more centralized control of the country's resources remained through the 1850s and into the 1860s. This need continued to provide fodder for political thought and political factionalism. Ultimately, Otto von Bismarck saw the way in which the world was going and created, essentially through a series of wars and domestic political tyranny, a unified Germany that quickly became a dominant world power. The trend towards nationalism, born of the economic stagnation of the mid-1800s, was in evidence everywhere, including (especially) in the United States with Lincoln's idea of a more unified, powerful America. The overall point is this: the economy once again demanded, relentlessly, *systemic* change.

That systemic changes come about violently means that the new dominant political thought becomes justification for nothing less than war. At these momentous times in history, political discourse dispenses with the minor issues of governance and cuts right to the very heart of government itself. What is its role? This is the question that continues to raise its head every four or five generations, brought about by the failure of the economic system the prevailing government has embraced.

An economic system is more than just one facet of a government. An economic system is the *reason* for a government. Societies form as humankind evolves, and societies themselves evolve into communities and cities and countries. Governments are instituted to protect the populace and to further enable its growth. But for a society to continue to develop, it must create wealth or value. For this, it requires resources, labor, and capital. These are the inputs of wealth creation. Simply put, prosperous societies need the ability to acquire, develop, allocate, manage, and secure these inputs, and then to regulate the results. Government is the consequence of these societal requirements. And it has become government's role, then, to ensure that these tasks are carried out. Governments, in short, derive power to implement and enforce some sort of order by which their societies may create value and prosper.

The question that keeps rearing its head is where, precisely, does this power get vested? Within the society, power can be vested in no one (an occupied territory, for instance, where the power is outside of the society) or it can be vested in everyone (pure democracy) or it can be vested somewhere in between.

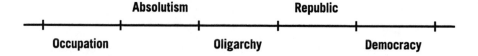

With the respective vesting come the attendant rights of the society's members. You can tell where you are on the spectrum by the individual's rights that are bestowed by the government. You won't find strong individual rights, for instance, in an occupied land.

From the power structure comes the system for governing the inputs and outputs of wealth creation – the acquisition and allocation, etc., of the country's resources. This is the economic system of the country and though each system might be different, they all try to perform the same tasks. Every economic system is concerned with the administration of the needs and products of wealth creation. And so within the continuum of power, we have the continuum of economies:

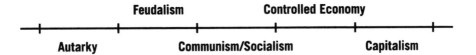

When a given economy stops administering the components of wealth creation effectively – as evidenced by economic crisis, low wealth creation, and rising inequality – the call goes forth from the populace to change the economic system. If the economic system remains unchanged by the prevailing power structure, then the call goes further. Change is demanded of the power structure itself.

Once that point is reached, the political discourse turns to the alternatives. Sides are chosen. Sometimes a single, significant opposing side, sometimes many opposing sides. It is at these times that political polarity takes on a life of its own. The political call for change becomes the proverbial rolling snowball. It can go in many directions, but the one direction it cannot go is back to where it began. The divisiveness becomes politicized and, of necessity, polarizing. The polarity leads to entrenchment. The entrenchment leads to conflict. The conflict starts within the society, but the search for resolution may extend far beyond its boundaries. Empire and Nationalism are familiar examples of this.

If there was political factionalism prior to the French Revolution (and other conflicts of the time, notably the American Revolution), and political factionalism prior to Bismarck and the Prussian wars (not to mention the American Civil War of the same period), nowhere in recent history was the political factionalism as widespread as it was prior to World War II. Factionalism not only scorched the political landscapes within societies but spread like wildfire, blackening virtually every nation.

The old order of Industrial Nationalism was faltering, and it began to take on radical new forms the world over. In its extreme was fascism, in evidence in Hitler's Germany and Mussolini's Italy. Japan's imperialism was yet another form of fascism. Japan had gained world prominence after World War I but had become mired in economic decline soon afterwards. The Japanese Showa recession of 1926 was soon followed by the worldwide depression of the 1930s and for Japan, as elsewhere, the crises led to dangerous political turmoil. Militarism grew in political strength as the Japanese population began to consider the tradition-rich military as its saving grace from the economic threats of the world in which it was now enmeshed.

Communism was growing in power as well. The Soviet Union appeared strong and became, to many on the outside, a model for a potential new economic system. It was not necessarily as admired by those on the inside. A famine in 1932-33 resulted in the deaths of millions in the Soviet Union. The *Holodomor* ("hungry mass death") was a consequence of natural causes but also the inefficiency of the forced collectivization of farms. But the news of the famine was suppressed. Speaking about it publically was a crime against the state. Not until the early 1990s, some sixty years after the fact, did the world learn about the *Holodomor*.

But the *Holodomor* took place, as we know, within a larger framework. Natural causes and inefficiencies notwithstanding, the world itself was in no position to economically handle a disaster of any magnitude. The Dust Bowl was proving that in the United States. The global economy was failing everywhere, and economic systems throughout the world were being questioned. The divisiveness was leading to incendiary political debate – the kind that moves people to take drastic action.

Communism was taking hold in China as well. And so, naturally, was political factionalism. The Communist Party of China had been formed back in 1919, not long after the Russian Revolution. By 1927, the CPC was at war with the nationalist government of the Republic of China. The Chinese Civil War would drag on ten years, take a hiatus when the two sides uneasily joined together to fight the Japanese during World War II, and resume in 1946 after Japan's defeat.

But perhaps nowhere was factionalism more instructive to regard than in Spain in 1936. That country, too, devolved into civil war. At its core, it was the Republicans, loyal to the government of the Spanish Republic, versus the Nationalist rebel group led by Francisco Franco. But in times of world-changing geopolitical divisiveness, things are never quite so simple. The Republicans, referring to themselves as the Loyalists, were a disparate mix of Marxists, anarchists, communists, and democrats. They received weapons from the Soviet Union and support from various volunteer groups around the globe including some from the United States. The Nationalists were fiercely anti-communist and pro-fascist, finding allies in Hitler and Mussolini. The former provided armored units and Luftwaffe planes and the latter supplied men. Hitler, in fact, used the opportunity to test his military's technology as well as the rest of Europe's resolve. Great Britain and France, confused over which side to support (in a somewhat analogous situation to today's Syrian civil war), stayed on the sidelines, a position that did not go unnoticed by the German Fuhrer.

Even in the U.S., stable by the standards of Europe in the 1930s, there was riotous factionalism. The stock market crash of 1929 was hailed by communists as the start of capitalism's long-anticipated demise. But there were plenty of other groups presenting alternatives to the nation's economic and (therefore) political system. There were socialists. There were trade unionists. There were anarchists. There were left-wing groups that split from the communist party on ideological grounds. There were social fascists. There were the Wobblies – the International Workers of the World, bent on creating "One Big Union" of the world's labor class. There was the German American Federation with its goal of encouraging American support for Nazi Germany. There were all manner of radical organizations and of course there were the New Dealers. Franklin Delano Roosevelt's plan for pulling the country out of the Great Depression was radical in and of itself.

What's significant is not that these factions existed. Some had been formed decades earlier. What's significant is the level of credibility they started to achieve. One couldn't rightly call them mainstream (except of course for those embracing FDR's New Deal policies), but they were no longer necessarily relegated to the fringe, either. Their messages were getting through because the world was ready to hear new messages. Things were not working anymore, in the U.S. and everywhere. The input and the output of the world's resources, labor, and capital were no longer being administered effectively. Collectively, the economic systems of the world were failing. And with that failure came the collective failure of governmental systems, of the world order. All that was left was for the factions representing the available alternatives to battle it out.

World War II came in chaos, more extreme than ever seen before, or at least not seen since the time of the Thirty Years' War. The Spanish Civil War provided a microcosm of what the world was going to see. The level of dissonance seen in Spain was multiplied the world over. And it created the conditions for war in and of itself but also because it enabled the emboldening of those who saw in the dissonance the opportunity to strike. When majorities are hard to come by, when it is difficult if not impossible to get huge masses of people to move in any single direction, desperate belligerents with desperate followings can wreak havoc. So it was with Hitler who surely saw opportunity when he witnessed the inertia of Europe – France and Great Britain in particular – during the Spanish Civil War. United States factionalism must certainly have been regarded as weakness by the Japanese in December of 1941. It's worth considering whether we are seeing this even now in Eastern Europe and in the Middle East. Those opposed to the U.S. and the West must see the paralysis produced by the massive geopolitical polarity apparent today. Will those enemies of the West act on it? Are they acting on it now? It's also worth considering the consequences as demonstrated by history of attacking a nation in such a state. Nothing solidifies quite like an attack from outside. The Japanese greatly underestimated the cost of waking the sleeping (albeit splintered) giant.

So what political faction becomes the next order's mainstream? History shows it is always the faction that successfully solves the problems every other faction is trying unsuccessfully to solve. Of course it's never that apparent at the time. While order change is being undertaken, the concerns are rudimentary, even primitive. It's the economy. It's having food to eat. Lincoln and Bismarck and FDR may well have been thinking long-term, recognizing the underlying conditions that, in their times, were creating the lethal drag on the world's collective ability to creatively advance, and understanding therefore the need to eliminate those conditions. For everybody else, the issue was simpler: defending one's quality of life, if not life itself.

CHAPTER EIGHT

The Nature of Man and War

War is an ugly thing, but not the ugliest of things.
The decayed and degraded state of moral and patriotic feeling
which thinks that nothing is worth war is much worse.
JOHN STUART MILL

World order changes are historical hallmarks that are never seen at the time for what they are. The American revolutionaries might have sensed the import of their actions. Lincoln and Roosevelt, too. But even still, what was in store for the world at the respective times of those men could not possibly have been grasped even by them for the sheer momentous nature of it. And the men who answered the call to war and did the actual fighting on the battlefields could not have even begun to imagine the world-changing effects of their actions.

The wars that occur between world orders are global in scope, though they may take different forms. The beginning of the Self-Determination order, for instance, was marked by revolutions. The beginning of Nationalism was marked by civil wars and other wars for unification. The beginning of the Superpower order was marked by world wars. But all of the wars in each respective period were global in their collective reach and fought for the same reasons.

But if those reasons were not recognized for what they fundamentally were at the time (to effect world order change), then why *do* people go to war? Why does one nation fight another nation? Why do people within nations conduct civil war? What is it that propels people into such seemingly desperate, lethal decisions?

In 1943, Abraham Maslow published "A Theory of Human Motivation" in *Psychological Review* which outlined his now famous hierarchy of human needs, represented by the chart below. Though the theory itself has come under varied criticism over the years, it's generally agreed that certain needs do indeed appear to be universal. Maslow's overall point seems commonsensical enough. At the bottom of his pyramid are the most basic of needs, and as one's needs are met and one is freed from the daily grind of having to seek the fulfillment of them, one begins moving on to more

Maslow's Hierarchy of Needs

complex objectives, culminating in self-actualizing activities.

Societies form essentially as mechanisms for meeting the basic needs of safety and security. Communities come together to help fill the need for love and belonging. Governments are established. With these more fundamental needs taken care of, the populace is freed up for the higher pursuits.

In geopolitical terms, problems arise when the citizens of a nation begin to feel as though their lower needs are not being met – if their safety and security, homes, bank accounts, and very lives appear to be under threat. At this point, a society's collective peace of mind is replaced with a heightened sense of anxiety, even dread. Something is no longer working. Such a tenuous circumstance cannot continue for very long without action being taken – by the government or by the people – to alleviate the perceived threat. It's a leap, of course, to say that the resulting action will necessarily be war. But it's important to recognize that *if* the course of action is war, it is because of this threat to basic needs. And historically, we can see that the leap typically consists of failed attempts to rid the threat in peaceful ways, leaving the one last resort.

Consider two societies. If there are abundant resources and opportunities for both, the pressures for competition between the societies will be relatively low. Greed, of course, could become a factor, prompting one society to compete for more than a fair share, but the expected benefit resulting from further success decreases as the costs of the competition grow higher. Sooner or later, the members of the succeeding society will give up competing, the gain not worth the pain.

If resource and opportunity are sufficient for one society but not both, each society will compete for such, the importance of the resource or opportunity to the survival of the societies determining the level of competition, with war being at the highest level.

If there is insufficient resource and opportunity for both

societies, then the societies will break up into smaller groups and compete amongst the other groups until there is a successful group of sufficient size given the amount of resource and opportunity.

This is not to say that there aren't other (ostensible) reasons besides not getting one's basic needs met for why people go to war. There may be one or more of a variety of stated causes of any given war and those causes may have to do with ideological factors (the crusades in the late Middle Ages or freeing the slaves in the Civil War) or perhaps struggles for power (Napoleon, Hitler) or perhaps a conflict over resources (any number of wars). But it might be noted that at the very base of the conflict, in most any historical example one wants to point to, one group had something another group perceived it *needed* for itself.

Ideological reasons for going to war are therefore often ancillary to the true purpose. Yes, the Civil War was fought to free the slaves, but it was also fought with an eye towards the industrial future of the world's economy and the fear of America being left behind. The Revolutionary War was fought for independence, but nobody complained about British rule until said rule began laying its claim to the colonists' pocketbooks through onerous taxation. The same thing happened in France where freedom was the rallying cry but the main concern was having enough bread to eat ("Let them eat cake," Marie Antoinette famously never really said). Power grabs by those at the top are often made not for some noble nationalistic purpose but to assuage the masses at the bottom (e.g., Germans suffering through their catastrophic economic times of the 1920s and '30s).

Yet even in times of suffering, war is mostly held as the final recourse. Particularly in terms of global wars, many steps are first undertaken to avoid the catastrophe of war. Consequently, many things have to go wrong. Negotiations fail. Or perhaps one side fails to live up to some prior accord; maybe circumstances have made it impossible for them to do so. Oftentimes the cost-benefit perception of war is skewed away from reality. It's probably safe to say that the amount of carnage and destruction in every major war was underestimated (sometimes vastly so) by the participants going in. "You will be home before the leaves have fallen from the trees," Kaiser Wilhelm II told his troops in August 1914. Similar statements are made in every war. Who could have foreseen the devastation and scope of World War II? Who could have predicted Hiroshima in a world in which atomic weaponry did not even exist? At other times, the government simply doesn't properly represent the inclinations of its people. Russia had the manpower in World War I, but quickly lost the will to fight "the Tsar's war."

All of which is to say that many things have to go awry before war is waged. Many things have to line up just so. And it is this that makes war, especially global war, so unbelievable, so unforeseeable. Surely, it is thought, reason will prevail and peace will reign. War always comes as a shock.

One prerequisite for war must be a general consensus of the people waging it that it is in some sense a "just" war. Perhaps it is waged for an ideological reason as mentioned above. Perhaps it is waged in the name of self-defense. Self-defense is justified for war and self-defense is justified as a means by which to purportedly hinder war. Military build-ups are based on this justification and often huge sectors of a nation's economy are devoted to it. The United States military-industrial complex comes to mind, but history is replete with countries building militaries in the presumed hope they will never have to be used. Whether the strategy is valid is debatable, but one can't help but be reminded of Anton Chekhov's famous principle that if a pistol is introduced in the first act of a play, one can be sure it will be used by the third. In any event, war is always justified in some way and after it is over, it is justified, especially by and for the victors. Few Americans would argue that the Revolutionary War, the Civil War, and World War II were not worth fighting.

How can we see that war is coming? Is there a way to make its appearance less of a surprise, a way to reveal its imminence sooner? Maybe even, by so doing, prevent it? What are the signs? The Carnegie Commission on Preventing Deadly Conflict has produced perhaps the most respected list of early-warning indicators of war, including demographic pressures (rapid changes in population, for example), severe economic distress, massive human flight (refugees pouring out of a country), and other bellwethers of imminent conflict. Yet, it's reasonable to wonder if these indicators help us much beyond identifying the symptoms of a conflicted world or some conflicted part of the world. Throughout history we can see one or more of them in every conflict, and we can see some of them even now. The question is whether we can do something about what we are seeing.

On a global level, these indicators produce that sense of heightened tension, that anxious sense of unease. But what produces the indicators? If characteristics of looming war are present on a more worldwide basis, if we see several of them at once in different hotspots, we can be reasonably certain that something must be shifting in the very order of the world. Demographic pressures, human rights violations, economic distress, multitudes of refugees – these are all the hallmarks of shifts in the global balance of power. The world witnessed these hallmarks when Absolutism turned towards Self-Determination, when Self-Determination turned towards Nationalism, and when Nationalism turned towards the order of the Superpowers.

In each case, we also saw something else – economic conditions of significant financial inequality. This inequality created divisiveness and exacerbated the anxiety caused by the shift in the world order. It's a perfect storm of sorts – a world in a great state of flux and significant economic problems to boot. And it is here that we are returned inevitably to Maslow. On an individual basis, safety, security, and well-being are threatened, if not outright destroyed. When this path is taken to its logical conclusion, and when those steps undertaken to avoid war fail, the world is pushed to a kind of no-return point. The proverbial immovable object verses the unstoppable force. Something has to give and the giving is always violent. It is at this juncture that a group (or groups) comes to the conclusion that the benefit of going to war will exceed the cost of the current state of affairs. Very simply, they cannot accept their circumstances any longer and become willing to sacrifice whatever peace exists to change them.

If there's any hope then of ridding the world of war, it must come much earlier than the point at which we begin seeing the financial inequality and subsequent divisiveness that lead to the Carnegie indicators. The time to stop war is at that point where the productivity cycle that is part and parcel of the world order begins its downswing. This, after all, is the point in which financial inequality begins to build its irreversible momentum. But because the downswing is a result of the unavoidable burning out of an upswing and has a tendency to go undetected anyway, perhaps the only way to avoid a global catastrophe is to eliminate the cycle altogether; flatten it out, in other words. Create an economic environment where productivity levels neither rise nor fall. But to do this, everyone in the world would have to act in concert. Perfect information would be required, including perfect insight into the actions and consequences of all of earth's seven billion inhabitants. Only by pooling the collective knowledge of the world's population could the uneven nature of progress be removed. For it is the lack of this information and insight that creates the randomness, the uncertainty, and the unintended consequences that lead to the peaks and valleys and fits and starts of the path of humankind.

In other words, it's the *condition of humanity* that leads inevitably to war. We are a species with imperfect knowledge, subject to a never-ending "butterfly effect" of changing and unpredictable circumstances. A tiny change *here* creates, in time, a significant change *there*. And it is this very unpredictability that causes in man a self-preserving desire to try to control the only thing he can – possibly – control: his immediate environment. We work, that is to say, for self-interest. This, by necessity, is the nature of man, and therefore the nature of war.

The human condition is that of imperfection. We are seemingly driven almost exclusively by love and fear, both of which are often misplaced. We love the wrong things (things, that is to say, that eventually prove harmful to us), and we fear either unnecessarily or insufficiently. Our emotions skew our vision of reality. We chase money or power or status. We are moved by hate or envy. At our best, we can be compassionate, but our sympathies can often cause us to move in errant directions. We can be disciplined, but we can also be lazy and indifferent. We can be careful and cautious in seeking change, but we can just as easily be impulsive and reckless. We often see and hear only what we want to see and hear. We try to balance our needs with the needs of loved ones, and sometimes we fail. We try to look ahead, but for the most part we can only see that which is right in front of us. We fumble our way through a life that is absent an instruction book. We learn through experience, but often we forget its lessons.

We are human. We are unpredictable. Moreover, we seem to like it that way. We chafe at regimentation and predictability and the confines of a life without risk. We push the envelope.

It's what moves us. All of this creates a world of inescapable conflict. Seven billion people not moving in unison, but instead randomly bumping into each other on their imperfect paths. Randomness, in other words, is the one sure thing. Perhaps the only truly predictable phenomenon is the fluctuating nature of our productivity cycle.

What this all means is that, collectively, people will always end up, no matter the starting point, in relative inequality. Once unequal, momentum builds. Those who do well acquire the wherewithal to do better. Those who do poorly lose that wherewithal. The world eventually moves towards a divisive state of those with and those without. And periodically, this rift of divisiveness must be settled. The failing order must be replaced by a new order that will allow for the resumption of productivity and wealth creation. It's a cleaning of the slate. A resetting of the clock.

Even if we were to somehow remove the concept of productivity itself from the equation, the sequence would be unchanged. To remove productivity would mean having to remove the demand for productivity. If we want for nothing, there is nothing for which to fight. Can a world be envisioned of people living peacefully off the land, a never-changing society of life lived at its most basic, most primal level? It would be a life of mere survival. It would be Eden before the fall. Perhaps the real fall of man, if one wishes to characterize it as such, had less to do with forbidden fruit and more to do with a desire for growth and betterment and creativity, the desire for a life lived above the level of survival. Maslow's need for self-actualizing pursuits. There were, at one time, hunter-gatherer societies, but these societies developed into agrarian societies and agrarian societies developed into ever more sophisticated cultures, complete with art and music and cathedrals and factories and automobiles and telephones and jet planes and rocket ships to the moon.

No matter how basic we're willing to make our lives, sooner or later, somebody's going to figure out a way to pick potatoes faster or build a stronger shelter. And others will copy that way. And improve upon it. And the race will be on. It is our very destiny. We cannot, as a species, remain still. It's not war that's an inherent part of our nature. It's imagination.

From the dawn of civilization, humankind has made huge productive strides. The strides have never been steady, but have come in waves, bettering life until the inevitable, and unavoidable, overreach and resulting downturn. What has followed the downturns represents the worst moments of history. But there has never been a way around them. The fuel of greatly productive times will always burn itself out eventually and the fall will be a hard one. When it reaches the point where one group's very way of life becomes threatened, it will – rather predictably – become a violent one.

CHAPTER NINE

EXHIBIT 1:
The Rise of the Monarchs
(1648)

War made the state, and the state made war.
CHARLES TILLY

Arthur Tudor died at the age of sixteen from an unknown illness.

Just six months prior, Arthur had been wed, but the marriage had never been consummated, his widow was quick to point out. Therefore, according to the laws of the Church, the marriage was never valid. This allowed the widow to marry Arthur's brother Henry, which both sets of parents supported whole-heartedly.

Arthur and Henry's father was Henry VII, King of England. And the King's interest in seeing Henry marry Arthur's widow came from his desire to continue the alliance he was nurturing with Spain. The widow, Catherine of Aragon, was the daughter of Spain's King Ferdinand II and Queen Isabella.

Stubbornly refusing to marry Catherine for seven years, the younger Henry finally relented in 1509 shortly after taking the throne upon his father's death. Now, with the responsibility of being king, Henry VIII understood the consequence of the alliance and the import of marriage to Catherine. He declared that he would honor his father's dying wish.

But Henry had not been without marital options. Also available to him had been the granddaughter of Holy Roman Emperor Maximilian I. There was a time when the Holy Roman Empire was one of the most powerful states in Europe, enjoying its symbiotic relationship with the powerful Roman Catholic Church, a relationship that went back to the coronation of Charlemagne as Emperor by Pope Leo III on Christmas day of the year 800. The bond essentially gave the Church unrivaled military and political power, a nation to do its earthly bidding.

A direct link to Maximilian might have seemed an irresistible prize for Henry. But by then, the Church and the Empire was in decline. An association with Spain became far more attractive. Henry no doubt had been captivated by the Spanish monarchs, who were succeeding in their quest for wealth and power. Capitalizing on new scientific discoveries and leveraging their own strategic relationship with the Church, Ferdinand and Isabella had been effectively underwriting the exploration and plunder of the New World. Moreover, the Spanish naval fleet, dominant in the Atlantic and Mediterranean, had become the envy of all of the European monarchs. An alliance with the decrepit, landlocked Holy Roman Empire could not have held nearly the same sway. It became clear to Henry that marrying Catherine of Aragon was the wisest choice.

The popular legacy of Henry VIII is, of course, the story of his many wives, a legacy that is often used (correctly) to explain his break from the Roman Catholic Church. But

Henry's true role in history far exceeds the matter of his marriages. King Henry VIII was one of the key protagonists in the world order shift from the Church to Absolutism under the European monarchs, and his actions would have significant implications on the directions the world would take centuries later. Not only would Henry influence the Reformation of the Church, he would begin to steer England on a course towards the formation of the American colonies and the grander British Empire.

Leading up to the time of Henry, the Roman Catholic Church had unquestionably been the world's most powerful institution. From its modest beginnings with the life and crucifixion of Jesus, the Church ultimately became the guiding force that would fill the vacuum created by the Roman Empire's demise and lead the way for Europe out of the Dark Ages. Europe settled into an efficient system whereby powerful landowners offered security to the masses in exchange for their production from the land. The Church regulated this value-creating feudal system through each party's ties to the Catholic religion. The pope would influence the landowners (the lords) and the clergy would see to the masses. With the Church as general partner and the lords as limited partners, this system would change the face of not only Europe, but the world as well.

Feudalism nurtured a return to productivity and wealth creation that had not been seen since the era of Rome. New stability allowed for prosperity and growth. Fewer resources were spent on defense and job specialization ensued. Instead of only farmers and fighters, now there were blacksmiths, carpenters, cobblers, bakers, masons, tailors, and brewers. No longer fleeing as nomads from threat to threat, the peasants stayed within the safety of the lord's manor. Towns sprang up, organized farming and livestock production yielded an abundance of food, people lived longer, and birth rates increased. Market economies developed with barter, trade, and coinage. And finally, the clergy had a lasting flock to tend to. Parishes with large congregations supported the clergy and churches began to dot the countryside.

The lords accumulated vast amounts of new wealth and competition ensued amongst this rising noble class. The hierarchy of the privileged evolved with a pecking order full of gentlemen, knights, barons, counts, dukes, princes, and ultimately kings. Manors expanded to shires, shires to counties, and counties to kingdoms. As these territories were organized, roads and other infrastructure were developed or expanded. Flying buttresses and arches marked the development of gothic architecture and huge cathedrals were constructed, all built to the greater glory of God.

Guilds of craftsmen formed as the free exchange of labor and services, along with the population boom, helped drive the world's economy to unprecedented levels. Commerce thrived. European trade between states and with faraway places grew dramatically. Wilderness areas were cleared to make way for new cities and the rising populations. Inventions included cranes, the wheelbarrow, the paper mill, the vertical windmill, spectacles, the blast furnace, and the wine press.

Religious orders of priests and monks such as the Benedictines, the Franciscans, the Dominicans, and the Jesuits built abbeys and the abbeys formed mini-ecosystems by themselves. Cathedrals, hospitals, and schools sprang up supported by the Church or its religious orders. The High Middle Ages saw the world's first universities established. Institutions with their roots in Christian monastic schools were created in France, Spain, Italy, and England. Theology was studied in the universities, of course, but so were medicine, law, and various arts. It was an intellectual revival and it led to advances in science and mathematics. Needless to say, a significant portion of Europe's newfound productivity and wealth creation made its way to the Church's treasury.

There were other forms of feudalism in Asia and the Middle East as well, but none were nearly as influential to the course of world history as the European system. And the major difference was primarily attributable to the Church. The Church was good for feudalism, and feudalism was good for the Church.

The Church, at the height of its power, was the glue that held the European system together. The Catholic belief was a powerful force. It gave the pope and the Church power to evoke its will on both the nobles and the peasants. The clergy controlled the peasants with the promise of an afterlife and the administering of the sacraments. The Church's leadership controlled the nobles with its influence over their wealth and stature. Catholicism was a requirement of nobility and the Church had the ultimate power to appoint, sanction, and excommunicate the nobles.

But change would inevitably come, and the story of King Henry VIII represents a precursor and a perfect microcosm of the world's transformation. Henry was intent on moving on from the dictates of the Church, believing that it was necessary to advance his own cause and extend the power of his state. If Henry felt this, in a larger sense the world must have felt it too.

Typical of the European monarchs at the time, Henry was a devout Catholic. In fact, in 1521 Henry published "Assertio Septem Sacramentorum" ("Defense of the Seven Sacraments") for which Pope Leo X bestowed on him the title *Fidei Defensor* (Defender of the Faith). One of the central themes of the work was in support of papal supremacy.

But the relationship between Henry and the Church had not been without its trials. Previously, Pope Julius II had baited Henry with promises of the French monarchy in exchange for his military support in the pope's conflict with

France in 1511. The fascination of another coronation complete with the title of "Most Christian King of France" had been as a Siren luring Henry toward the Normandy coast. But Henry came out on the losing side, his coffers seriously depleted and his dreams of the French throne crashed on the shore.

Meanwhile, Henry's plans for a strategic alliance with Spain had also failed. Queen Catherine's relatives had been less than willing to share the spoils of New World discoveries, and Catherine had been unable to provide Henry with a male heir. Although she'd become pregnant by Henry six times, only one child – Mary – survived infancy. Henry needed to protect the lineage of the House of Tudor. And that meant he needed a son. Worse for Catherine, Henry had become enamored with one Anne Boleyn. He petitioned to the Church to have his marriage annulled.

For Henry, there were reasons for the annulment that went beyond even Catherine's failure to provide him an heir or his desire for Anne. Geopolitical reasons. With the unfolding competition for wealth and power over the New World, Henry knew he could no longer be tied to Spain, either through marriage or progeny. Henry's vision for England was for dominance in the Americas and control of the Atlantic. Neither was possible if England was connected or subordinated to an already dominant Spain. Catherine's link to Spain was no longer valuable and, without being able to provide him a son, neither was she. Catherine was a connection that needed to be broken.

Pope Clement VII, the only one able to grant such an annulment, respectfully declined. It wasn't that Clement was necessarily against the granting of annulments. They were granted to royalty quite often. But typically, the granting was a *quid pro quo*. King Louis XII of France, for example, was given an annulment but only in return for military support for the pope. But Henry's relationship with the Church was strained to the point where he was unwilling and unable to offer anything sufficient to gain the pope's acquiescence.

Meanwhile, the monarchs of the Holy Roman Empire and Spain agreed with Pope Clement. The Holy Roman Emperor, Charles V, happened to be Catherine's nephew, and it was clearly within Spain's best interest to maintain a blood relationship to the English throne. Charles had no desire to see his aunt cast aside from the English court. The bedfellows of the pope and the monarchs loyal to the Holy See were ready to impede the gathering power of England in any way possible.

Further, the pope was not in a position to contradict the wishes of his royal supporters even if he had wanted to. The Church had already lost power to many of the European monarchs and specifically, at that time, Clement had come under direct assault by Italian states that no longer respected divine papal authority. Military support from Spain and the Holy Roman Empire was needed to defend the papacy. Henry's coveted annulment was out of the question.

And so began the English Reformation. Henry would take matters into his own hands, and by his doing would come the final chapters of the world order that had been dominated by the Church.

Henry's solution to what became known as the king's "great matter" was simple. If the pope wouldn't grant him his annulment, he'd simply remove the pope from the equation. In fact, he'd remove the Church from the equation, splitting the Church of England from the Roman Catholic Church and making himself the Church of England's Supreme Head. Such drastic measures must have been unanticipated by the pope. There was no precedent for a major Catholic monarch turning his back on the Church, and Henry's actions would represent a historic turning point in the course of the

Church's power.

But Henry's actions were symptomatic of the broader instability of the era. It was becoming a fitful time for all of the monarchs of Europe and a precarious time for the popes. The nobles were amassing wealth and power from the increasing productivity and advancement of the age. Possessing a desire for independence, but fettered by their allegiance to the Church and the popes, the French, English, and Spanish monarchs, and even the Holy Roman Emperor, found themselves with conflicting views on the heavenly derived power of the pope. Many, like Henry, had discovered firsthand that doing business with the pope was a losing proposition. The ill-fated crusades and other military forays at the Church's invitation, with their accompanying assurances of participation in the expansions around the Mediterranean, had not delivered the wealth and power that had been advertised. Consequently, the monarchs looked to the New World and over time, they would seek to distance themselves from the Church. But Henry's split from the Church was the first and most prominent.

The English Reformation was part of the larger Protestant Reformation in Europe. Shortly after Henry came to the English throne, Martin Luther had nailed his *Ninety-Five Theses on the Power and Efficacy of Indulgences* to the door of the Castle Church in Wittenberg. (Or so goes the legend. The truth is most likely much less romantic, with Luther sending the *Ninety-Five Theses* to some well-appointed Church leaders from where the work spread throughout Germany and then the rest of Europe.) A particularly significant consequence of the Protestant Reformation was that power was forced away from the Church and placed in the hands of kings. These kings would come to be believed as being divined by God and vested with absolute power.

To fill the void developing from the decline of the Church,

a fierce competitive rivalry was stoked between the major monarchies of the day, primarily England, France, and Spain. Seeking dominion of the new lands, the powers collectively would fuel an epic period of growth that would leave the Church behind.

But the Church's loss of power would be a gradual process. As human advancement continued to move beyond the feudal system that had been in place for centuries, the Church attempted to block the destined path. It was an impossible task. This was the same Church that was behind the failure of the Crusades, had no satisfactory answer for the Black Death, and was eschewing the new advances of science. The world continued to slip further and further from Church dogma as people began exploring the world in new ways. Scientifically, yes, but also philosophically, and, importantly, geographically. Developments in sailing and navigational technology helped to ignite the Age of Discovery, which led from exploration to colonization as Europeans fanned out to the New World and beyond. Vast new empires were to be built.

The ultimate transition of power from the Church to the Absolutism of the monarchs came about like every world order change – violently. As the old order failed, leaving the world in that rudderless state that naturally evolves when the world awaits a new order, along came the Thirty Years' War. Fought from 1618 to 1648, virtually all of Europe was involved including the Holy Roman Empire, England, France, Spain, and even the Russians and the Ottoman Empire. Though the war was primarily fought in what is today Germany, belligerents battled as far away as Asia, Africa, and the Americas. It was truly the world's first *world* war. And coming at a time of economic stagnation throughout Europe (the inevitable state of affairs between world orders), the war was devastating. The population in the German states was wiped out from anywhere between 25%-40%, up to two-thirds in some areas.

There were approximately eight million casualties of the war, a catastrophic 10% of Europe's entire population at the time.

The war resulted in the breaking apart of the Holy Roman Empire, but of course it was more than that. The Empire, a union of territories directed by an emperor laden with the power of the Pope, was losing its strength because it was losing its authority along with the Church. With its presumed connection to divinity now called into question by the Reformation, the multi-ethnic Empire could no longer hold, decentralizing into hundreds of kingdoms and fiefdoms and principalities, some small, some large. Those nations allied with the Empire and hanging on to the old order (most notably Spain) witnessed the loss of their power as well. Those opposed to breaking free of the status quo of the Church and the Holy Roman Empire (namely France) saw themselves rise to the status of new world order leader.

The war ended with the Peace of Westphalia in 1648, ushering in a new era of political order that recognized the sovereignty of nations, granting them their own authority, free from the interference of the Church. And all throughout Europe, that authority was now – by virtue of the spoils of war – in the hands of the respective monarchs. Westphalian Sovereignty has become a principle of international law used even today to describe the notion of non-interference between nations when it comes to their respective domestic affairs. The Peace of Westphalia, then, was a monumental turning point in the history of humankind, essentially defining the modern nation-state.

It was a brand new world and tremendous growth and wealth creation returned. From 1640 to 1690, the population of the American colonies quadrupled and the resources of the new lands created unprecedented wealth. Colonization soon led to mercantilism with the exports and imports of the colonies – thus their economies – controlled by the monarchs of the respective mother countries. It was an economic system that could not have developed under the Church.

The Westphalian legacy may or may not have been recognized at the time for what it was. What was most likely going through the minds of the delegations at Osnabrück and Münster, the cities where the treaties were signed, was that the Peace represented an end of conflict for as far into the future as one cared to look. With the matter of the world's power now settled, peace would reign. Of course disagreements were bound to come up in time, territorial disputes here and there. This was to be expected. But war such as had been seen for three long decades was now a thing of the past. The dominion of nations was established and the nations were led by the divine hands of kings and queens.

For most of Europe's inhabitants, it would have been impossible to imagine in their lifetimes that there would ever again be a need for the kind of catastrophic global conflict witnessed during the Thirty Years' War. Indeed, such was the case. Significant global warfare would not be witnessed again for approximately five generations with the start of Europe's Seven Years' War. And it would be this war, fought in the mid-1700s on most of the world's continents and oceans that would ultimately lead to the demise of the monarchs. The system of Absolutism, with its origins dating back to Henry VIII and his pursuit of an annulment, first from Catherine and then from the Roman Catholic Church, would reach its natural end.

CHAPTER TEN

EXHIBIT 2:
The Rise of Self-Determination (1776)

Destroying is a necessary function in life.
Everything has its season, and all things eventually
lose their effectiveness and die.
MARGARET J. WHEATLEY

There was a way of life before the steam engine, and there was a way of life after the steam engine. Rarely has there been such a dramatic divide in the history of humankind's progress. Before the implementation of steam power, goods were made by hand and transported by wagon or sail. Afterwards, mills and factories churned out goods that were moved by steamship and train. The Industrial Revolution swept the world and the end results included mass production, widely available goods, massive urbanization, a new middle class, and a higher overall standard of living. There were, of course, other contemporaneous inventions besides the steam engine, but for the late eighteenth century, James Watt's creation stands as the perfect symbol of the rapidly changing world.

Watt's development of the so-called atmospheric engine of Thomas Newcomen was so integral to the Industrial Revolution that Watt is often mistaken as the inventor of the steam engine. He was not. But his improvements to Newcomen's design were significant enough that Watt's engine was practically a new and different entity altogether. New and different enough to warrant patent protection. And as integral as the steam engine was to the Industrial Revolution, patent law was even more so.

Historians might debate the finer point of whether or not Watt's patent in particular (for "A New Invented Method of Lessening the Consumption of Steam and Fuel in Fire Engines") actually sped up the pace of the Industrial Revolution. Watt spent valuable time just defending his rights in court from others trying to improve on Newcomen's design, and then, for a time, he used his patent to effectively limit open access to his own design, thus driving up its price. But nobody denies the impact the steam engine itself had on the Industrial Revolution. It's impossible to image the Revolution without it. And it's also difficult to imagine that, without protection for one's own intellectual ideas, one would be as keen on investing one's time and money on the development and marketing of any invention, steam engine or otherwise. Incentivizing is an obvious reason patent law exists, after all.

But patent law, as it was in Watt's time, was relatively new. Early concepts of intellectual property rights evolved during the Italian Renaissance of the fifteenth century. Initial attempts at protecting intellectual property mostly failed, however, as innovations had (and continue to have) a tendency to be appropriated and even abused by the power structure in effect at the time. So it was at first with patent protection. During the sixteenth century, at the height of Absolutism, "letters patent" were bestowed only by the European monarchs and commonly limited to certain favored individuals. This essentially allowed royally chartered monopolies on key technologies. For a king, it was another means of sustaining his power, another way to extract value from the production of his kingdom. And the letters of patent often came with steep fees and effectively served as an additional form of taxation. In 1624, in an effort to curtail the monarch's power over patents, the English Parliament passed the Statute of Monopolies, which effectively wiped the slate clean on any prevailing monopolies previously granted by the monarchs. Going forward, new patents could be filed. Unfortunately, the statute became essentially worthless for new innovation; the courts that decided patent cases were still controlled by the monarchs.

Not until the next century (after the English Civil War) would patent law effectively be taken out of the hands of the monarchs. The loss was a harbinger of things to come and symbolized well the change in order that was beginning to take place. The monarchs were losing their control. And along with the loss of control came the dismantling of the monarch's divine right of absolute power. Monarchies would no longer be above the reproach of their subjects. "There is something exceedingly ridiculous in the composition of Monarchy," wrote Thomas Paine from across the Atlantic in his 1776 pamphlet *Common Sense*. "One of the strongest natural proofs of the folly of the hereditary right in kings is that nature disapproves it, otherwise she would not so frequently turn it into ridicule by giving mankind an ass for a lion." Paine, of course, was speaking about English monarchy in particular, and a war would be fought to separate the colonies from English rule.

But two-hundred and thirty years later, Great Britain still has her Queen. The world seems enamored by English royalty, in fact. Why? The answer may well go all the way back to

January 30, 1649. On that date, King Charles I, fervid believer in the divine right of kings (and famous serial abuser of the patent system of the Statute of Monopolies), spoke these words: "For the people – their liberty and their freedom consists in having government... It is not for having *share* in government, sirs, that is nothing pertaining to them. A subject and sovereign are clean different things." The people happened to disagree, evidenced by the fact that Charles's words were part of larger statement – his last speech – made on a scaffold erected in front of the Palace of Whitehall. A few moments later, he was beheaded.

Charles's execution, a culmination of the English Civil War, presaged the trend against the monarchs just at the time when the great monarchs of the world were coming into their own. The execution was just a year after the Peace of Westphalia, ending the Thirty Years' War. England, it would seem, was ahead of the curve. The people wanted more parliamentarian rule and less authoritarian "divinely-inspired" control over their lives. It would take more than a century, however, for the power of English royalty to completely give way to representative government. Charles II, after all, would restore the monarchy just eleven years after his father's execution. But it was never the same. And over time, power continued to shift away from the English royals, most notably during the rule of King George I (from 1714 to 1727) when true governmental authority resided less in the king's hands and more in the hands of Sir Robert Walpole, Britain's first *de facto* prime minister. And then the shift was punctuated by the reign of King George III (from 1760 to 1820) when the power of the monarch was further diminished not just within the country, but globally as well. The king's subjects may have still been willing to serve the king within Britain, but that sentiment no longer extended to America where the colonists had had enough kingly rule.

The power of British royalty, then, subsided slowly. So much so, that the country never bothered to completely do away with the Royal family, choosing instead to give them symbolic and ceremonial power and to continue, to this day, to revel in the grandeur that once was. Within the shores of England, there was no single defining moment since Charles II's restoration when royalty was the sudden villain and had to be done away with permanently. The kings and queens of Britain could see the writing on the wall. They knew that if they wanted to keep their positions, as well as their lives, they needed to cede their power.

After the Revolutionary War, King George III could certainly see the shift the world was taking. He needed to look no further than across the English Channel. Unlike England, power in France shifted violently between rule by monarch and representative government. Never was it more violent than the French Revolution which cost Louis XVI his head in 1789. In time, Napoleon would crown himself Emperor, the House of Bourbon would be overthrown, and Louis Phillipe would be forced to abdicate. But it was the Revolution that spelled the true end of continuous French monarchy. From that time forward, representative government was a force that could no longer be ignored.

In Spain, King Charles III, ruling from 1759 to 1788, noted the decline of his country, no doubt saw the decline in monarchical power all over Europe, and moved towards "enlightened absolutism," a kind of benevolent dictatorship. Charles tried to push Spain forward by diminishing the role of the Church, which had still been dragging Spain down from the world order prior, and he latched on to scientific advances and promoted agricultural modernization. He enjoyed some success and managed to maintain his power (and his head), but his successors fared not so well. Charles IV was forced to abdicate, as was Ferdinand VII after him.

Joseph I (installed by his brother Napoleon) followed Ferdinand and was deposed within a few years.

Some monarchs managed to hold on to their power in the mid-eighteenth century, but it wasn't necessarily an easy task. Catherine the Great of Russia reigned during what became known as Russia's Golden Age but nevertheless had to deal with the Cossack Rebellion of 1773-1775, the largest peasant rebellion in Russia's history. The royal power of Russia, too, would eventually wane, but disastrously in slow motion, Russia's revolution coming far too late to take advantage of the direction humankind had moved. The same could be said for Austria, Hungary, and the Ottoman Empire, and the fates of all these nations would ultimately be catastrophic because of the delay.

For the countries that were separating themselves from monarchical rule, huge leaps in advancement were the rewards. Watt's steam engine was born in Great Britain and so was the Industrial Revolution. This was hardly a coincidence. But the world's separation from the monarchs had actually been stoked years before it manifested. With mercantilism becoming the predominant economic system of the globe, a new class of capital holders grew. Commerce with the colonies created a need for traders, shippers, merchants, and investors. Where the bourgeois was once marked by royalty-sanctioned ownership of land, now it was marked by both land and capital, and capital was the resource becoming increasingly more valuable.

This shifted power from nobility to the individual, and the shift came with philosophical underpinnings that predated the order of Self-Determination by almost a century. Writing in his *Second Treatise of Government*, John Locke argued in 1689 that labor put forth in the utilization of property and resources – the creation of value – is what justifies ownership. This labor theory of value implied a right to property that supersedes government (think patent law). Thus, people are naturally independent and a person therefore has a right to defend his own "life, health, liberty, or possessions." Thomas Jefferson would echo these words when writing the Declaration of Independence eighty-seven years later. Locke also influenced French writers Voltaire and Rousseau who wrote of the sovereignty of the self, writings that, in turn, influenced other eighteenth-century thinkers. The idea of an individual's rights, upheld by representative government and not government by monarch or church or aristocracy, was beginning to find its footing. In the same year Jefferson wrote the Declaration, Adam Smith would write his magnum opus, *An Inquiry into the Nature and Causes of the Wealth of Nations*, an exposition on the fundamentals of economics and capitalism. By then, the words *laissez-faire* had come into the lexicon. (*"Laissez faire, telle devrait être la devise de toute puissance publique,"* wrote French statesman René-Louis d'Argenson: "Let it be, that should be the motto of all public powers.")

But it wouldn't be until individuals began acquiring wealth and power, through the shift of capital that mercantilism allowed for, that the idea of true individual rights (civil and economic) could become manifest. Now there was more than just a philosophical base for new power structures; there was a new class of people who no longer needed the monarchs. In the aggregate, the monarchs could no longer offer the world an environment conducive to progress, hindering humankind rather than advancing it. In fact, mercantilism itself, as a tool of the monarchs, soon became an obstacle to progress. In America, mercantilism had left the colonists with little say in trade arrangements. Seaports were monopolized by England and imports frequently came with high tariffs. Exports were often limited to England, too, significantly reducing the customer base of the American producers of goods.

In time, the colonists would gain significant control over

their trade, excluding Europe in general from the "trade triangle" that had been in place. European countries had traded finished goods for African slaves and then shipped the slaves to the Americas to be traded for cotton and other goods. The cotton would make its way back to Europe where it would be used in textile manufacturing, and then the finished products would be sent back down to Africa for more slaves. But the colonies began to cut out the European leg of the triangle: slaves would be sent to the Caribbean in exchange for molasses, which would be sent to New England where it would be distilled into rum and then sent to Africa to be traded for more slaves.

The profitability of mercantilism would continue to ebb for the European monarchs and the decline became more apparent as the economies of Europe began to suffer more and more, as economies do when the world order in place hits its inevitable outer boundary. In England, King George was drifting further and further into debt, exacerbated by the cost of the Seven Years' War. He would respond by exerting even more control over the colonists, issuing a series of fiats including the Currency Act in 1764, the Stamp Act in 1765, and the Quartering Act a month after the Stamp Act, all of which had the effect of severely hampering the economy of the colonies. The Stamp Act was repealed in 1766, but it was soon followed by a series of acts collectively known as the Townshend Acts, most of which were designed to raise revenue for Great Britain at the cost of the colonies.

Moreover, the colonies could not expand under British rule. The wealth created during the Age of Discovery was dwindling in the increasingly populated areas of the settled colonies, but an untold abundance of resource and opportunity was waiting to the west. Expansion, however, was something King George could no longer afford. Nor could he allow his colonists to usurp his authority by expanding without him. The western boundary of the American colonies became the perfect symbol of the boundary of the age of the monarchs.

One of the final straws for the American colonies was a tax on local tea, allowing the East India Tea Company to gain a monopoly on the colonies' tea trade. The Tea Act, which imposed the tax, was a response by the British parliament to help bail out East India, a British company that happened to owe the Bank of England money it could not pay back. The East India Tea Company had been hit hard by the Credit Crisis of 1772. From the mid-1760s, mercantilism had created an expansion of credit which resulted in an unsustainable financial boom. Exports increased dramatically to the colonies and nobody seemed especially concerned that the colonists were not buying a goodly portion of what was being shipped there. Credit expansion flowed to the southern planters as well, or at least to those in Britain who were investing in the planters. Supply continued to outstrip demand which led to lower revenues which led to a greater need for credit, a need the banks happily filled. But when it started to become clear that the notes couldn't be paid (the East India Tea Company a prime example), confidence in the banks fell rapidly. The resultant run on the banks caused twenty major British banking houses to sink into bankruptcy. Elsewhere in Europe, France continued to have its own problems, its government defaulting in 1770 and again in 1788. The order of the monarchs was working no longer.

The failures of the monarchs to provide for their subjects, coupled with the movement towards the sovereign rights of individuals, spelled the end of the world order of Absolutism. For Great Britain, the end began on the battlefields of Lexington and Concord in 1775. But in terms of the violent, global turmoil that accompanies all world order changes, the American Revolution was but the centerpiece. The Seven

Years' War ran as a precursor and the French Revolution followed. And then the Napoleonic Wars continued the revolutionary conflict of Europe, involving France, Russia, Great Britain, Austria, Hungary, Spain, Portugal, Prussia, the Ottoman Empire, the Papal States, and a host of other belligerent nations, most all of which were led by kings and queens. The friction between them represented the death throes of the monarchist system and if it came unanticipated, it should not have. "I think it impossible that the great monarchies of Europe can last much longer," Rousseau said to anybody who was listening, years before the storming of the Bastille.

The new world order that followed was reflected by representative government, individual rights, capitalism, and free enterprise. And for those countries that adapted to the new order, immense success would be the prize. The British (her kings and queens keeping their titles but willingly ceding power) and American societies best embodied these attributes and over the next half century they would economically outpace the other nations of the world that did not accept or only partially accepted the new path.

The new period of high growth and productivity around the turn of the nineteenth century brought the steam engine and a slew of other great advances in manufacturing, including the power loom and the cotton gin (both patented, of course). Unprecedented efficiencies in production, coupled with a transition from traditional sources of fuel, including wood, to more efficient and cost-effective coal, led to economic and social transformations that left no part of life untouched. Although some of the inventions of the Industrial Revolution had their origins in the 1700s, their industrial applications would be seen most conspicuously in the period from 1800 through 1830. Iron, cement, gas lighting, and even chemicals like sodium carbonate (used in the production of glass, paper, soap, and textiles) enjoyed widespread use.

The Industrial Revolution touched off a change in the culture of humankind that was without precedent. And without the shift to the individual of both capital and the rights thereto, none of it could have happened. None of it could have happened, that is to say, without the removal of the order of Absolutism.

But in time, the Industrial Revolution would stall. The order of Self-Determination would come up against its own boundaries. Humankind's creative evolution would be hindered by the very thing that stoked it after the fall of the monarchs. And once again, history would be poised to repeat itself. The benefits of the Industrial Revolution grew beyond the capacity and structure of the world order then in place. Self-Determination was failing and a new order was needed.

CHAPTER ELEVEN

EXHIBIT 3:
The Rise of Nationalism (1850s)

The statesman's task is to hear God's footsteps
marching through history, and to try and catch on to
His coattails as He marches past.
OTTO VON BISMARCK

In the United States, names like Carnegie, Rockefeller, Edison, and Ford defined the Second Industrial Revolution. But across the Atlantic, there were other names: Krupp, Daimler, and Benz, for example. Germany had its own share of inventors and industrialists. Huge German business concerns like BASF and Bayer were leading the world in chemical and pharmaceutical manufacturing. Towards the end of the nineteenth century, all of Germany was experiencing rapid industrial development propelled by a rich coal industry, extensive steel production, a fast-growing banking industry, and a rail system that was the envy of Europe.

And yet just a few decades earlier, Germany, with Prussia as its core, had been essentially nothing more than a loose confederation of states, existing more as a collection of principalities than as a unified country. But it was a collection linked by language, shared culture, and a history of defending itself against France's armies. What would drive the country towards unification, what would drive it to become one of the two preeminent industrial powers of the world, would be the visionary leadership of Otto Von Bismarck.

Bismarck at one time would have seemed an unlikely candidate for the role. He'd been raised a Junker, as Prussia's land-owning nobility were known. And in 1848, during the Year of Revolution in Europe, it was the conservative Junkers who were in the crosshairs of the revolutionaries. But Bismarck perceived what was at stake and what was ultimately possible for a greater Germany and he knew that if change was coming, it needed to be for the right reasons and in the right direction. "If there is to be a revolution," he said, "we would rather make it, than suffer it."

The direction, Bismarck knew, was towards a greater, culturally unified German region with a strong central government. This had been the collective call of the crowds in 1848 – demand for a national structure that would give power to the German peoples. It was a call Bismarck would answer, understanding as he did that the wealth and power of the German states had been left untapped by its disjointed configuration. The development of that wealth and power, under a united Germanic realm, would allow Germany to compete with, even dominate, the great powers of the world.

It was a call, in other words, for Nationalism. The order of Self-Determination was dying and its death was coming with all the usual symptoms of economic burnout, financial inequality, turmoil, and divisiveness. In their current forms, governments were inadequate in their capacity to generate prosperity for their people. The technologies from the First Industrial Revolution now demanded access to major resources, the marshalling of which required entities much more powerful than individuals or the corporate structures of individuals. And to capitalize on the mass production developed in the first half of the nineteenth century, huge new consumer markets had to be developed under common control. Governments themselves needed to step back into the picture to fully capture the new efficiencies. But this time, not as monarchies with absolute power, but as facilitators and directors creating an environment conducive to even further growth.

Earlier attempts at German unification had failed. But Bismarck, appointed to his office in 1862 by King Wilhelm I, wasted little time in outlining a new vision of unification to the Prussian Chamber of Deputies: "Prussia must concentrate and maintain its power for the favorable moment which has already slipped by several times. Prussia's boundaries according to the [Congress of] Vienna treaties are not favorable to a healthy state life. The great questions of the time will not be resolved by speeches and majority decisions – but by iron and blood."

The Congress of Vienna treaties that Bismarck was rejecting were anachronisms, agreed to in 1814-1815 by Britain, Russia, Austria, and Prussia. The purpose was to create a balance of power throughout Europe in the wake of the Napoleonic Wars. Revolutionary France had proven to the major powers that demands for the civil and economic liberties that the order of Self-Determination was bringing into the world were impractical and dangerous to the status quo. But it was a move backwards, restoring power to the monarchies and nobilities and aristocracies that ran the age of Absolutism. The notable exception was Great Britain, which was weaning itself off royal power while also extricating itself from continental entanglements. For the rest of Europe, it was reckoned that going back to the old ways would mean stability could be achieved again. Stability came at a price, in other words, and the price was the liberties and economic rights made possible by the new order of Self-Determination. Coming out of the Congress of Vienna, the Conservative Order, as the movement became known, emphasized tradition and deference to central authority typified by the old order of absolute monarchs.

The Congress, joined eventually by France, was successful for a time. Warfare between the major nations was limited. But notwithstanding the direction the Conservative Order preferred for the world, the First Industrial Revolution moved it in another. Proof rested with Great Britain, but also across the Atlantic, where the United States was becoming a world power through industrialization and representative democracy. This was the way of growth. A century before, in the Age of Discovery, growth came by way of expansion. The great powers colonized and reigned over their empires with armed might. But those days were over. Especially so with a continental treaty in place for the purpose of maintaining a military balance of power. Competition between the great nations of the world shifted from war to industry out of necessity.

Otto Von Bismarck saw the future – the direction of the new order – and broke free of the Vienna Congress and unified Germany. The Crimean War of 1853-1856 between Russia and the Ottoman Empire (the latter joined in alliance by France and Great Britain) effectively broke the Congress anyway, giving Bismarck justification. The Austro-Prussian War of 1866 and the Franco-Prussian War of 1870-1871 created the powerful unified Germany the "Iron Chancellor" sought. It was a new empire – a German *Reich*. And by the turn of the twentieth century, the country, led by a powerful combination of government and industry, became the economic leader of Europe and, along with the United States, an architect of the Second Industrial Revolution.

Unification wasn't limited to Germany. The 1848 revolts stoked a movement towards the nationalistic consolidation of Italian states as well. Split up and presided over mostly by Austria, with the Papal States reigning in Rome and protected in part by Napoleon III, two wars of independence would be fought before the birth of the Kingdom of Italy in 1861. A third would be fought in 1866 to further unify the new nation. Ultimately, with Napoleon III forced to recall his troops from Rome for use in the Franco-Prussian War, Rome would become the Kingdom's new capital.

In Russia, the call was not so much nationalism as it was modernization. Russian had been badly defeated in the Crimean War after having expanded towards the Black Sea, threatening the Ottomans. Facing a restless populace in the precarious financial times of the 1850s, the expansion southward had been a necessity for the Tsar. A warm water port would boost the Russian economy by better promoting year-round trade. But the war, probably most famous today for the medical service of Florence Nightingale as well as Tennyson's poem about the charge of the Light Brigade at the Battle of Balaclava ("Into the valley of death rode the six hundred…"), revealed just how far the Russians were behind the rest of Europe. The Ottomans were backed by both the French and British (both seeking to maintain Europe's balance of power), and the latter had shown up on the battlefield with weaponry the Russians could not match. Russia, still with its outdated monarchy, had unwittingly insulated itself from the advances of industrialization. Russia's economy was predominantly agrarian and it was a system that unbelievably still included serfs. Humiliated by the war and suddenly aware of his empire's backward ways, Alexander II instituted a number of economic reforms, although none of them would ultimately be sufficient for Russia to catch up with the rest of Europe.

Chief among the Tsar's reforms was the abolition of the serfs with the Emancipation Manifesto of 1861. If that sounds familiar, it's because something remarkably similar was playing out at the same time in the United States where the system at issue wasn't serfdom, but slavery. Abraham Lincoln's Emancipation Proclamation came just two years after Alexander's Manifesto. But for the United States, only part of the nation had been mired in outdated agrarian ways: the South. Still, it was enough. In an age of rising industrial nationalism, Lincoln no doubt knew that the South's antiquated economy, along with its regional self-interest, was going to impede the U.S. economic and industrial potential.

By then, the economic evidence of the decline of the order of Self-Determination was ample. The Panic of 1825, a stock market crash causing bank failures in England was an early signal that the economic rise due to the Industrial Revolution had reached its peak. But economic expansion still appeared to be fully underway in the 1830s, stoked by debt-induced growth in the United States, in particular. In time, however, the growth fell off. Like most times of slowing growth, nobody initially noticed. Expansion continued – fueled by more debt. But when the Bank of England raised interest rates as a response to its decline in monetary reserves, banks in New York were forced to follow suit. And the sudden tightening of credit led to falling prices, plummeting profits, and the Panic of 1837, which sunk the U.S. into a recession that wouldn't end until the mid-1840s.

Shortly thereafter, another financial panic ensued. This one was caused specifically by the U.S. railroad industry boom, a boom that had been fueled in large part by borrowed money. State and territorial governments in the unsettled West provided incentives to the railroads by granting them rights of eminent domain and bestowing them with needed financing. These governments borrowed along with the railroads, all betting on the future growth of the West. But the West at that point was only beginning to become settled. Migration had been a trickle. The transcontinental railway (propelled by the Civil War) was two decades away. Pacific coast civilization was connected only by shipping routes around South America's Cape Horn and wagon train through dangerous and uncharted territory. Investors were not dissuaded. By 1850, nine thousand miles of track had been laid out west, some of it leading virtually to nowhere. Ironically, the American railroad boom was enjoyed most keenly in Great Britain, where American railroad stock fueled a bullish stock market. The inexorable bust was also felt most keenly in Great Britain when the London financial markets began to collapse in 1847, the repercussions of which helped fuel the 1848 revolts throughout Europe.

If the Panic of 1837 was suffered mostly by the United States, and the Panic of 1847 mostly by Great Britain, the Panic of 1857 was a more worldwide phenomenon, mostly because the world was a far more connected place by then through advances achieved in transportation. Economic prosperity in the U.S. in the 1850s led, as par for the course, to overexpansion in a number of industries, including the aforementioned railroad industry in no small way. When migration, such as it was at that time, began to slow, so did the profits of the railroad companies. Land prices in the West were doomed to fall as well. The ensuing chain of events created an economic downturn on a national level, then a global one. Investments that didn't seem risky when they were made suddenly became lethal in the plummeting economy. And, once again, banks failed. When a huge one – the Ohio Life Insurance and Trust Company – succumbed in

August of 1857, the panic went into full throttle.

The industrial American North was hit hard by the Panic of 1857. Businesses failed, unemployment rose to record levels, stocks crashed, and displaced laborers rioted. Interestingly, the South remained relatively unscathed. "Cotton is King," declared South Carolina Senator James Henry Hammond in 1858, noting that the demand for southern cotton remained high even in the worst of economic times. The Panic of 1857 highlighted the economic sectionalism between the North and the South. The two economies were driven by two distinctly different – and incompatible – interests. It was an economic house divided that, in a few short years, would not stand.

The Panic gave the South what would become a false sense of security, a mistaken validation of their economy. The North, like the rest of the advancing world, was mechanizing not only its manufacturing industries but its agriculture. By 1860, the North would have twice the value of farm machinery as the South and would produce 80% of the nation's wheat. The wealth of the South, meanwhile, would continue to be driven almost entirely by their slave economy.

Resentment for the South increased in the North, exacerbated by the Dred Scott decision of 1857 (which, in turn, exacerbated the Panic). The Supreme Court ruled that Congress did not have the authority to prohibit slavery in the territories that had joined the nation since its creation, thus opening the door for the western territories to become slave states with free labor with which the northeast industrialists could not compete. Moreover, new slave states in the West meant access to resources – gold and silver – for the South.

Many historians have surmised that Lincoln must have known the Dred Scott decision was going to place the U.S. on a course toward civil war. While not an abolitionist himself, Lincoln knew that Southern slavery was inconsistent with the ideals the nation was founded upon and that the great social experiment of American democracy could never endure unless the inconsistency was removed. The North and South, forged into a nation four generations before by the Revolutionary War, had been growing increasingly dissimilar since, and now dangerously so. But it's been suggested that Lincoln was a believer, as were many by the 1850s, that slavery would fall of its own accord, a victim of politics and economics. Lincoln saw the world moving toward industrial dominance. Slavery could never survive the transformative changes brought about by the Industrial Revolution. Moreover, the political power and industries of the North would soon dominate the vast new resources of the West. The South would continue to slide backwards into economic isolation.

Lincoln, however, most likely had not expected the outcome of Dred Scott. Any hope for slavery's imminent (non-violent) demise was seemingly ended. The South's potential dominance over Western wealth meant the North would have to act. Mineral extraction, settlement of the land, and the building of infrastructure could open new frontiers for slavery, breathing new life into the South. The threat to the Union and the American ideals of equality, individual rights, and government of the people would find new strength and not just wither away. And Lincoln's worldview of a unified nation, under a strong federal government, with its unlimited potential for growth and prosperity in an industrialized world, was now at risk. Slavery had to be exorcised, the South needed to be pushed forward, and the nation – and its resources – needed to remain united.

The showdown cost the lives of 600,000, by far the deadliest of all the wars leading to the rise of Nationalism. But the end result of all the mid-nineteenth century wars of revolution and unification was a new world order that replaced the failing order of Self-Determination and allowed for humankind's creativity to advance once more from where it had become mired.

The technological advances from 1870 through the beginning of the twentieth century were unprecedented. And so was the growth of the global economy. The Second Industrial Revolution was marked by centralized governments with power sufficient to cross boundaries of states or provinces, even nations, allowing for real growth of railroads and the spread of telegraph lines and electricity. For the U.S. in particular, mega projects backed by the government included the Panama Canal. It was an age of progress that could not have come about in a world of small, decentralized governments. Like Absolutism before it, Self-Determination had reached its limits.

If the new order marked by strong nations with federal governments allowed for economic growth, it also allowed for the growth of their militaries, backed by fervent nationalistic pride. Relative peace was maintained for a time, with territorial expansion coming by way of treaties and alliances. But when the Second Industrial Revolution began to sputter, and the resources of the world order started to become more elusive, nations needed to fan out even more. But what was needed was a system that was not yet in place – a system of globalization, a system that would come about in time but was not possible during the era of Nationalism. The alliances at the beginning of the twentieth century were shaky. The interests of the world's great nations were in conflict. Trust was in short supply. And the armies kept growing.

Bismarck, who never lost his visionary abilities, warned of the coming storm. Reflecting on Prussia having been beaten by Napoleon twenty years after the death of Prussia's Frederick the Great, Bismarck remarked to Kaiser Wilhelm II, "The crash will come twenty years after my departure." Then, a year before he died in 1898, Bismarck is reported to have said, "One day the great European War will come out of some damned foolish thing in the Balkans." Seventeen years later, Archduke Franz Ferdinand was assassinated in Bosnia by a Serbian rebel, touching off World War I. Almost exactly twenty years after Bismarck's death, just as he'd predicted, Kaiser Wilhelm II, the last German Emperor, was forced to abdicate. The world order of Nationalism was finally being pushed aside. But it would take another quarter century, with crippling worldwide economic distress and not one but two world wars and wars in between, before it would finally be snuffed out.

CHAPTER TWELVE

The Day the Music Died

The inevitable is no less a shock just because it is inevitable.
JAMAICA KINCAID

What's it like when world orders begin their descent? The period leading up to a world order's ultimate demise, from just after the order peaks until war comes – what does that look like and how does it unfold? The events over the last quarter century are signaling that the Superpower world order, born from the ruins of Nationalism, is now in its decline. Is history set to repeat itself again?

In 1991, when the Soviet Union fell, the world changed gears. Capitalism won. A "peace dividend" created by a redirection of money away from defense spending infused cash into the Western economy. Eastern Europe continued its path towards greater market freedoms. Factories popped up seemingly overnight everywhere, Asia in particular. Capital flowed into Indonesia, Korea, Malaysia, the Philippines, and Thailand. China became a major player. The U.S. response was to outsource manufacturing and exportable services to the new low cost providers. This made more than just good business sense. The fact is, productivity and wealth creation was slowing in the U.S. Finding lower cost providers was necessary to maintaining an expected growing standard of living.

It was the start of a new collective business model, one that was very much different than the system in place when both superpowers were in play. The rest of the world would now do the low-value work, the labor-based jobs that Americans presumably didn't want anyway. Naturally the displaced blue-collar (and even white-collar service) workers weren't exactly thrilled with the direction, but the vision of the political leadership coupled with global economics made it impossible for the non-competitive jobs to stay in America. The economy of the United States, already tending toward a service orientation and away from a manufacturing one, became full-bore service based.

What that would eventually mean could be seen in a kind of microcosm way in the mid-'90s in Japan, had anyone bothered to make the connection. Japan, a manufacturing powerhouse in the 1970s and '80s, specializing in cars and electronics, found its economy beginning to falter. Land and stock prices fell steeply. Caused primarily by overextension, the declines were exacerbated by the new competition in the other Asian markets. The Japanese business model was being hijacked, and the Japanese couldn't compete with the cheap new capacity being created in China and Southeast Asia. It would be a harbinger of things to come.

Japan's overextension eventually would be followed throughout Asia. The money that had poured into the Asian countries for capital investment during their meteoric rise (the "Asian Economic Miracle" was what everybody had been calling it), created, before long, the inevitable overcapacity. The "Asian Flu" financial crisis of 1997 led to sinking Asian economies and plummeting currency values. Through U.S.-

led monetary stimulus, the markets recovered, but only temporarily. Soon, the fall in demand meant lower overall consumption and a fall in prices for energy and production-related commodities. Russia, heavily dependent on oil production, could not meet its government obligations and defaulted in 1998, creating further economic turmoil.

What happened exactly? Why were the new capitalistic nations of the world suddenly struggling? Where was the demand for the results of their productivity? Americans were certainly doing their part. U.S. consumers were importing seemingly everything from everywhere. Europeans, too, were on a buying spree. But the money that flowed into the emerging economies was not spent in turn. Asian countries produced. They made profits. But the profits didn't go to the workers. What the countries were producing, in other words, was everything but *consumers.* They saved their profits and lent them back to the U.S. and Europe to buy even more goods. U.S. and European debt increased. The Asian economies were giving the Western consumers more and more rope with which to hang themselves. But in the course of doing so, they ramped up to productive levels that went well beyond a sustainable level of demand.

Still, casting aside the natural mechanisms of supply and demand, the U.S. felt it was in its best interest to keep the other economies humming. After all, if the emerging economies of the new capitalistic world failed, what would that say about the U.S. Cold War victory? For the previous fifty years, we had been preaching our way of life. Now we were swamped with the newly converted. The problem was the church wasn't big enough to hold them all. The new period of *Pax Americana* meant that the United States international business model had become dependent on the success of foreign economies.

The model had looked very attractive in theory. We'd

been able to outsource much of our industrial capacity to instead rely on growth from clean, upscale, technologically driven business. As for the rest of the world, we'd prepared to be their bankers and consultants and managers. We would supply the foreign factories with technology to succeed. We'd profit by their success, and they'd provide us with cheap goods. And so the United States had to keep the model going. The U.S. committed to economic policies designed to stabilize the emerging economies by providing the necessary consumption, overproduction be damned. But the theory was all based upon a stable global society, not one that was on the verge of a global wealth creation slowdown and definitely not one with the seeds of widespread divisiveness planted by a global rise in financial inequality.

At first, all seemed well. The structural weakness of the global economy was hardly noticed. Something else was going on at the time that kept the weakness hidden. By the late 1990s, almost half a trillion dollars was flowing into the coffers of U.S. technology companies to take care of a potential computer glitch that became known as the Y2K problem. The practice of using two digits to represent the calendar year meant that computers were going to recognize 2000 as "00," causing havoc with the digital systems of the world and creating the potential for a halt in computer operations everywhere, a halt to life as we knew it. The spending that took place on account of this one-time event meant a cumulative increase in GDP of around 5% for the three years leading up to 2000. It gave the world a false sense of security. The U.S. economy looked robust. It was not. Once the effect of the Y2K stimulus passed, the world went into a recession.

But as the 1990s came to an end, money continued to be easily accessible, mostly through the savings glut created by the lack of spending by the emerging foreign economies. That money was making its way into the U.S., becoming more and more widely available as credit. Poor oversight of Fannie Mae and Freddie Mac, the unregulated shadow banking system, and recent global banking deregulation (more on each in a bit), all conspired to intensify the availability into the early 2000s. All were a result of the political desire to keep the economy chugging forward, and especially so in the face of the 2001 recession. The end of the Y2K period meant the slowing of capital investment in technology. It also meant, though few noticed, that the technology capacity that had been created for the Y2K problem was no longer relevant. And then of course overinvestment in tech companies led to the dot-com bubble and subsequent bust.

Something else was happening, too. The attacks of 9/11 were thrusting the U.S. and its Western allies into a war on terror that would ultimately lead to Afghanistan and then Iraq. The war on terror was creating huge bills that had to be paid. The world, and especially the U.S., couldn't afford a long recession. Easy credit and expansion of the money supply continued to mark U.S. economic and geopolitical policy and the rest of the world was more than accommodating.

Of course it all led to the subprime mortgage crisis of 2008. It's easy to trace the roots looking back. Fannie Mae and Freddie Mac (the Federal National Mortgage Association and the Federal Home Loan Corporation) were originally created as secondary mortgage markets, buying mortgages from banks and thereby allowing the banks to lend out even more money. The mission was simple: to promote home ownership across America. For decades, these government-sponsored entities worked just fine. But through the Housing and Community Development Act of 1992, as well as pressure by Congress and the Clinton administration in the late '90s, the road of good intentions led to a marked difference in the profile of home ownership. Mortgages started being under-written for low-income housing, and ownership climbed as the income of the average homeowner fell. Whereas just below two-thirds of American households owned houses before the 1990s, by 2007 close to 70% of households owned homes. This added up to approximately five million houses that were built and financed that probably should not have been. And with the growing rise of financial inequality, the additional number of households financing home ownership turned out to be a big move in the wrong direction.

Meanwhile, the global savings glut continued to escalate and the U.S. mortgage market responded with more popular delusion. Foreign investment (notably from the Chinese) in U.S. Treasury securities had driven down yields and exhausted the U.S. government securities market. Money shifted towards the only other market big enough to handle the glut of savings – the mortgage market. This created tremendous pressure on banks and other mortgage originators to generate more and more loans. Underwriting standards slipped and a private-label securitization market grew – the so-called shadow banking system that flew under the regulators' radar. Easy mortgage money meant, of course, high home values. The median price of a house in Los Angeles rose 170% between 2000 and 2006. This was an obvious symptom that something was seriously amiss. But who was watching?

As for the banking world itself, the safety valves that had been put in place during the Great Depression to mitigate risk were being largely undone. Why? Because from 1960 to 1990, the United States went from having six of the ten largest banks in the world to having none in the top twenty five. We had lost our banking superiority. This was deemed unacceptable for the leading nation of the free world, and since the fall of the Soviet Union, that world had become even bigger. We'd already lost (albeit willingly) our unofficial title of manufacturer to the world. We couldn't jeopardize our new role as financial manager of the world. To compete on the global stage, it was decided that a level of deregulation would be necessary. The Clinton administration pushed for the repeal of certain measures and for the first time in over fifty years, banks could, among other things, cross interstate lines, engage in the business of insurance and securities, and easily dispose of assets from their balance sheets through the use of colla-terized debt obligations. Banks no longer had to retain a significant portion of the risks related to mortgages, enabling them to reload their portfolios over and over. What it all meant was that money became easier and easier to borrow. And the country went deeper and deeper into debt.

International financial regulations became problematic as well. Global cooperation among international regulators came together with the Basel II Accord in 2004, outlining capital requirements for banks around the world that were based in large part on the rated strength of their investment portfolios. It was good in theory and intent. But the tendency of human nature to skirt the rules was overlooked. Financial engineers made the creation of assets that would meet the rating requirements into an art form. Managers were com-pensated for structuring financial products that were, in reality, much riskier than their ratings implied.

Meanwhile, the sudden competitive power of the banks meant that securities brokerage firms, which didn't have the luxury of funding their borrowings with customer deposits carrying the FDIC guarantee, had to take on major new risks in order to compete. Firms like Lehman Brothers, Bear Stearns, and Merrill Lynch took on dicey, imprudent invest-ments with higher leverage. In time, they would become financial casualties of their own overreach. And the only ones that could economically take on the portfolios of the fallen investment banks were the commercial banks that had the federally subsidized FDIC guarantee.

If one needed more proof that money was awash from

debt, one could note the proliferation of high-risk hedge funds throughout the '90s and into the 2000s. In 1990, there were less than a thousand of them. By 2008, it was estimated that over 10,000 hedge funds were in existence with over two trillion dollars of investment money.

But the hedge funds fared much better during the mortgage crisis than banks and securities brokerage firms. Many had "short" positions in place to hedge against their exposure. Seeing the writing on the wall, they shorted the housing and mortgage markets, making money as those markets dove downward.

But not everyone noticed the writing on the wall. The Federal Reserve was content to keep interest rates low, adding fuel to the fire. For Alan Greenspan, Chairman of the Fed, the circumstances of the '90s in particular presented something of a conundrum. Standard measures of productivity were down, yet profitability was up. Historically, profit increases due to productivity gains, but America was not producing more automobiles, mining more efficiently, or inventing any new major state of the art technology. Indeed, domestic companies lacked any real evidence of increased productivity. Yet spending was up and so were profits. Greenspan publically declared that we must have been entering a "new paradigm." In reality, there was nothing new about it. Spending and profits were up on borrowed money.

The graph below illustrates the economic crises of the last two decades, all of which relate to amount of debt relative to the level of actual wealth creation.

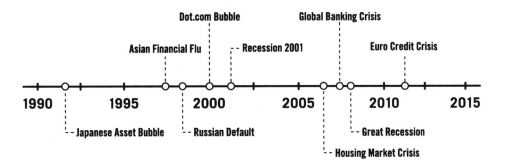

Recent Decades of Financial Crisis

In hindsight, everything that was done policy-wise (or not done, as the case may be), was because of one very simple dynamic: wealth creation was down. Policies were put in place that were reactions to the initial symptoms of the global decline in wealth creation, but those policies were effectively causing the money supply to increase, forcing more debt into the system and further exacerbating the problem of too much debt in a system relative to the amount of wealth that was being produced on a global basis. The decrease in productivity and wealth creation came about as the technology from the Cold War days – the Space Race, the Digital Age – was peaking and slowing with only marginal advancements.

Today, with no new significant technologies in which to invest, corporations are hoarding their cash. Investment is and has been critically low. The graph below shows what has happened to United States capital investment as a percentage of GDP. Note the drop from a high of over 22% in 1984 to a low of less than 15% in 2009, weakly rebounding to slightly over 16% in 2013. Currently, capital investment as a percentage of GDP has still not regained its historical average of over 20%.

U.S. Domestic Private Investment % of Total GDP

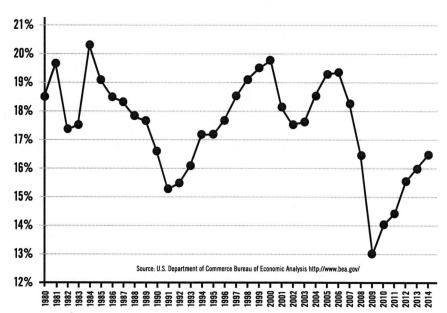

Source: U.S. Department of Commerce Bureau of Economic Analysis http://www.bea.gov/

Investment is one of the three major components of GDP. Consumption and government spending are the other two. If investment drops, which it clearly has, the only way to maintain the level of GDP is to increase consumption or increase government spending, or both. But such increases generally come only by way of debt. And in an environment with an already substantial level of debt, the increases can be disastrous.

Absent productive technological innovation in which to invest, what remains is investment in the new service-oriented economy. But service-oriented industries don't require huge outlays of capital. A distribution center for Wal-Mart doesn't require the type of investment required to build an automobile factory. How drastic is this changeover from manufacturing to service? Consider the Dow Jones Industrial Average. Historically, it was composed primarily of manufacturing companies. Innovators. Producers of goods. This makeup continued until the 1990s when things began to shift. Today, most of the Dow Jones companies are service and consumer oriented. Companies like American Express, Verizon, Mc-Donalds, and Wal-Mart now populate the Dow. It's the same with the Fortune 500. Financial services, product distributors, and services companies rule the American economy. Of the 27 million jobs created from 1990 to 2008, 98% were within the service sector of the economy.

Maybe it would be instructive to illustrate the problem with an allegory. Imagine, if you will, three towns: Town A, Town B, and Town C. Town A gained its wealth from lumber, Town B gained its wealth from oil, and Town C gained its wealth from steel. All the towns traded with each other, and all the towns did well. But Town C became so wealthy that many of its residents didn't want to work in the steel industry anymore. It was dangerous, labor-intensive work, after all, and the steel mills were unsightly. Town C took its wealth and invested it not in capital investment to keep its steel mills up-to-date and efficient, but instead in the lumber and oil businesses of Towns A and B.

Steel, meanwhile, began to be provided by the up-and-coming Town D. Town C was fine with this since Town C was now making money – lots of money – on its investments in the industries of the other towns. The businesses in Town C were now mostly comprised of companies that catered to the town's investors – dining establishments, car washes, hair salons, fitness centers, etc.

Eventually, Towns A, B, and D reached their maximum amount of production of lumber and oil and steel. Town C's investors began to lose money. No worries. Comfortable with their lifestyle and reluctant to give it up, they simply borrowed the money from the other towns, pledging their previously earned wealth and their investments as collateral. Of course, in time, the other towns were forced to halt their lending to Town C as the value of the collateral no longer supported the amounts Town C had borrowed. Soon, Town C experienced tremendous economic hardship.

Worse, it was too late to change the economic model back. Even if Town C had wanted to retool its steel mills, it had no money to do so. Plus, it had lost its skilled workforce by then. The other towns, having invested in manufacturing technology including the education of their workers, had passed Town C by. At this point, outsourcing to the other towns was all that Town C could possibly do. Soon, the investors in Town C went bankrupt and the service establishments that supported them went out of business right along with them.

Towns A, B, and D, meanwhile, lost a huge buyer of their products when Town C hit the proverbial skids, in addition to losing a significant source of financing. The ramifications reverberated throughout all the towns.

The point of the story is simple. When an economy that represents a significant chunk of the world's economic stage surrenders its manufacturing by becoming dependent on foreign industry, it surrenders its economic well-being as well. Not-so-incidentally, it also divides its populace in the process. There are the investors, the bankers, the hedge fund managers, the consultants, the high-tech financial engineers – and there are the people who serve them. The waiters and the hair dressers and the store clerks. What used to be the middle class is lost. What remains are the haves and the have-nots.

When the Cold War ended, the flood gates of globalization opened. The fact is we couldn't stop the outsourcing even if we had wanted to. The Cold War, an impediment to free markets and free trade for half the world's inhabitants, was removed. To put it into our allegory, Town C willingly gave its labor to the other towns, but it would have lost it anyway through the forces of the marketplace. All that Town C could do was hope the other towns would become consumers of their own products so Town C could thereby continue to reap the rewards of its investments. This is what didn't happen in the real world. Cultures steeped in histories of conservative consumer spending could not change overnight. And even if they had, it's unrealistic to assume cell phones made by Chinese laborers and purchased by Chinese consumers would continue to be made for the benefit of American and not Chinese corporate profits.

What happened was this: the world order as we knew it ended. And what we have seen since 1991, unfolding in front of our eyes, reveals all we need to know about the desperation created by the absence of wealth creation – the wealth that was created in a world that no longer exists. To replace the drop, governments have been doing what governments always do. They keep the flow of money going, which is to say they allow – create is not too strong a word – more and more bone-crushing debt. It is a natural political, natural *human*, response – defer the pain as long as possible.

And so it becomes worthwhile to ask what can be done at this point in our economic history to halt the slide, to reverse course, to stop the economic calamity and the consequences of it that we have seen in past historical periods – namely, the global conflict. What do you do with a failing economy?

CHAPTER THIRTEEN

What Do You Do with a Failing Economy?

We do not really know what causes economic growth. We do have a good sense of what are the main obstacles to growth and what are the conditions without which an economy can't grow. But we are far less sure about what are the other ingredients needed to create and sustain growth.

FRANÇOIS BOURGUIGNON, CHIEF ECONOMIST
AT THE WORLD BANK.

The fundamental problem with program maintenance is that fixing a defect has a substantial chance of introducing another.
FREDERICK P. BROOKS, JR.

Economies face many different types of challenges. There are banking crises, currency devaluations, runaway inflation, asset bubbles, stock market crashes, cyclical recessions, government defaults, and outright depressions. Usually when problems occur, it's a combination thereof.

The common denominator of all economic crises is that something, somewhere, is out of balance. In any given financial crisis, the economy is in some way out of equilibrium. There is too much or too little of something. Maybe there's too much production or too much consumption. Too little credit. Too much credit. Not enough investment. Too much investment. Too much government spending. Not enough spending on research and development. Moreover, not only can economies be out of sync, but even just a widespread *belief* that an economy is out of sync can result in a self-fulfilling outcome.

Considered a science, the application of economics is actually more like abstract art. Economic policymakers continually tinker with the right recipe for a successful economy. The ultimate aim should be to ensure a system that provides jobs and opportunity for advancement, allows for affordable products and services, and offers growth and stability. But if the global economic environment and the productivity cycles are out of sync, these objectives may be very hard or even impossible to achieve. Since policymakers cannot possibly determine all of the ramifications of their actions, some experts argue that even making the attempt to artificially manage an economy is fruitless at best and, at worst, fraught with blowback consequences.

Even economists will admit that it is (in Alan Greenspan's words) "devilishly difficult" to accurately measure the components of an economy as complex as, say, the economy of the United States. But even smaller economies are complex and measurements are just as challenging, further hindered in many cases by the difficulties of gathering accurate information in the first place. What this means is that on a global level, imbalances are hard to identify, hard to accurately make sense of, and virtually impossible to correct without causing further imbalances elsewhere.

When crises occur, politicians often mobilize frantically, attempting to treat the symptoms without thoroughly understanding and addressing the true underlying causes. Understandably, they want to alleviate the pain to their constituency. But their efforts can be misguided, ineffective, and can actually exacerbate the problem. And because financial crises unfold as symptoms of imbalances, and because distinguishing the causes from the symptoms is imprecise, any attempted correction is bound to become a politically charged process. If, for example, widespread bank failures occur, blame may be placed on the banks for not holding enough in reserves, even though the level of reserves may have been more than adequate over the several preceding decades. Perhaps the real reason for the crisis is an excessive amount of credit in the economy encouraged by government policy to inflate the money supply. Then the symptom (the bank failures) may be blamed while the cause (excessive money supply) escapes culpability.

Sometimes a financial crisis might not be indicative of what's really happening with the longer term trend of the underlying global economy. A sudden rise in oil prices or a series of corporate defaults in a particular industry, perhaps. Or some type of short-term market correction. The stock market crash of 1987 is a good example. At first it looked like another 1929-type crash in scale but the market recovered rapidly because the overall economy was in a period of high productivity. The stock market crash was essentially unconnected from what was happening in the grander scheme.

A financial crisis can also be limited to a specific region or country. Take for example the Latin American debt crisis of the 1980s. Countries like Argentina, Mexico, and Brazil couldn't pay their debts. In 1991, India witnessed a currency crisis related to their imbalance of imports versus exports. That crisis would go on to change their national business model. In the years after, India's economy transitioned toward much higher exports as part of the world's move towards more and more outsourcing and globalization. But neither crisis had any significant effect on the underlying global economy taken as a whole.

And then there are those troublesome cyclical recessions that routinely come about every five to seven years. When these types of recessions occur, jobs are lost and hardship is felt by a large segment of the population. But generally, these are only transitory pauses in the overall trend of upward growth. Something has moved out of balance temporarily, and the short pause gives the economy a chance to move back into equilibrium.

Thus when financial crisis strikes, a key question must be asked and answered: Is the financial crisis in question related to a truly isolated or temporary imbalance, or is it a symptom of a more serious systemic problem?

Since the systemic "dam breaks" are hard to predict and identify and tend to happen rarely (only every four or five generations), policymakers tend to discount the occurrence of a widespread systemic failure. How can they not? Prior to the crisis, even if the failure could be spotted on the horizon, politicians would be reluctant to do anything about it. The actions required would go against the grain of popular support. As long as the economy is showing signs of growth, why put the brakes on a seemingly good thing? And once the crisis starts, nobody wants to play the role of Chicken Little. Inciting fear carries too much risk of self-fulfilling behavioral reaction. Besides, what if the crisis is not of the systemic variety but instead a temporary imbalance? There is huge political risk in proclaiming the sky is falling when it may not be. In 2005, for example, many policymakers and prognosticators were suggesting the housing market was overheated. But they missed the fact that the overheating was related to a systemic failure rather than a temporary oversupply. Or did they? If their assertions had been fully vetted, their negative outlook may have either been scoffed at, or their concerns could have incited enough fear to be the tipping point of the sell-off that did eventually follow. It was a no-win situation.

It's easy to understand that, when most financial crises occur, they're dealt with, at least in the initial stages, as more common isolated problems. But there's also a human predisposition to underestimate the downside of any problem. The prevailing general belief is that it can't be that bad. Leadership becomes hesitant to paint a dire picture because of the potential for hopelessness and the negative feedback loop. And then the downward spiral begins to escalate. When the crisis situation fails to improve, reality sets in, panic rises, and steps to resolve the crisis are desperately pursued. Unfortunately, by then, the time to have changed the course has long since passed.

A true systemic failure is widespread and does not respect national boundaries, especially when national economies are well connected. It's not limited to an aberrant condition or to a specific place. Those cases, as we've discussed, are more representative of temporary imbalances. A short recession, a transitory plunge in the stock market – these are typically corrections. A temporary imbalance will heal much like a cold or the flu. A true systemic failure, on the other hand – a worldwide, persistent crisis – is a cancerous tumor on the global economy. But it's important to remember that a crisis is not the disease itself. Just as a tumor is not the cancer but rather a manifestation of the cancer, neither is the crisis the underlying problem. It's a symptom of the underlying problem, a symptom of a diseased economy. And the underlying problem of a diseased economy is always the lack of sufficient wealth creation.

Whether an individual government can actually help a

nation pull itself out of a global systemic crisis is a matter of some debate. Even if it's possible, there's the matter of just what to do – which strategies to follow and which economic tools to use. This often requires an impossibly predictive sense of where the economy is headed and what its potentials are. We discussed in Chapter 4 the problematic nature of gathering accurate economic data. And history reveals that even with accurate data, economies don't always act predictably, mostly because people don't act predictably. Human psychology can have an enormous impact on an economy. Emotions like fear or greed – what John Maynard Keynes famously called "animal spirits" – often dictate behavior in ways no amount of data can project. Stock markets can rise on nothing but human voracity and whole economies can stall from lack of confidence.

History has also shown that the most destructive financial crises, the global systemic failures that result in depression or near depression, are always the result of too much debt relative to the real wealth creation or productivity in the global economy. Excessive debt is not only the most destructive imbalance, but it is also the most onerous problem for an economy to solve. This is particularly true when the problem is happening simultaneously throughout most of the world's economies.

When wealth creation lags, thereby putting pressure on the standard of living, a typical response by both policymakers and economic participants is to increase debt and place reliance on unknown future opportunity. In this way, the standard of living doesn't suffer. The money supply is increased and excessive consumption is encouraged. Soon, of course, asset bubbles start to form. Yet there is a natural tendency to continue to increase the debt until it surpasses some unknown and dangerous boundary. If the crisis was caused by debt initially and then further debt is added, the stage is set for the proverbial house of cards, doomed to eventual collapse unless there is a definitive shift in the economy's productivity possibilities. Excessive debt can only be cleanly resolved by increasing wealth creation.

Other solutions may be attempted – austerity programs, currency devaluation, widespread defaults, or appropriating wealth from some source outside the economy – but each have accompanying problems and each can only shift the pain or delay the inevitable. And as with most problems, delay only makes the ultimate resolution more costly.

Unfortunately, economic strategies of policymakers to create wealth have their own limitations. First, no matter the strategy, there are no guarantees. An economy is like a business. It has risk. Profit is hoped for, but failure is always a possibility. Over the last three decades, central banks have portrayed an image as that of "maestro," conducting the economy faultlessly to perform as they intend. But of course their infallibility is a fiction, their credibility particularly strained in the case of global systemic failure. "Don't fight the Fed" is often repeated. But central banks have made and will continue to make mistakes. Even if the central banks' actions are correct, they can only shift or delay the pain until either "new shoots" of economic growth appear, for which the central banks have very little direct control, or their strategies become ineffectual or depleted prior to the return of productivity. Hopefully something happens before their tool boxes empty.

Second, wealth creation, as opposed to consumptive stimulus, takes time. The effort required for increasing wealth is much like piloting an enormous ship; there's a delay before the ship responds to even a hard turn of the wheel. When dealing with a society in economic crisis, time is not an affordable luxury.

Third, the foremost driver of new wealth creation is creativity. But creativity is the domain of the populace, not the government. The government can only provide the environment for creativity and remove the impediments that restrict it. Governments can set the goals and pave the way, but the mass of individuals must be free and have the support to come up with new ways of doing things. The NASA space program, exploration of the New World, the defeat of fascism – these were all programs achieved by individuals with the help of the government. The government cannot force creativity and new wealth creation.

Fourth, wealth creation usually requires capital investment now. When an economy is already reeling from lack of resources to cover its debt, redirecting those resources into capital investment can be difficult if not impossible. Some point to an abundance of funds sitting on the sidelines, able to rush into the game on short notice. But those funds are a result of the massive inflation of the money supply (as a result of more debt) and should they become available, it would mean more risk-taking in an already leveraged, high-risk environment. There's a reason why those funds are sitting on the sidelines.

Finally, along with this last point, there must be sufficient opportunity to make the capital investments worthwhile and meaningful to the entire economy. Because the economy was lacking in true productive endeavor before the crisis, it can be argued that worthwhile investment opportunities were insufficient then. What has changed since? One of the defining characteristics of a healthy investment environment is investments competing for money and not the other way around. In today's situation, we see a surplus of money chasing less than worthwhile investment.

In short, governmental attempts to generate new wealth are not viable solutions in the short term or long term. Not only are they insufficient to alleviate current economic pain, they are fraught with ramifications that may make matters worse. And so policymakers continue borrowing against anticipated future wealth as this becomes the only available course. The goal is to maintain a status quo that slips further and further away. Preserving the standard of living (consumption) becomes the highest priority. The hope and prayer is that future productivity gains will eventually kick in and exceed later growth expectations, thereby providing the ability to pay back the advance that has been taken. Will the tide turn before the economy's borrowing capacity is exhausted? The unknowns, of course, are *if* and *when* the required productivity will result. It's a gambler betting double or nothing, hoping for the big payoff, hoping his luck turns before the chips run out.

The Japanese financial crisis of the 1990s was a harbinger of the problems the world has faced in the decades after. It was a symptom, a crack in the dam of global net productivity. The Japanese instituted policies similar to those above, thinking that the tide would shift and productivity would return to levels more in line with what was seen in the 1980s. But the Japanese failed to anticipate that China and other emerging economies would emulate the Japanese business model, making it impossible for the Japanese to regain their past export dominance. Consequently, the Japanese have been waiting for productivity to kick in for a very long time. Even if new underlying productivity and wealth creation does return for Japan, net economic growth will remain stunted; the benefits of the productivity will be muted by the burden of debt, and for a long time to come. What is striking (and troubling) in the Japanese situation is the fact that Japan's policymakers have pursued a wide array of strategies for recovery and none have worked. Japan's only real solution is to change their business model for the world's new operating environment. But that would be mean removing impediments and wholesale change to their status quo, an exceedingly difficult proposition.

Rather than such wholesale change, governments, unable to create wealth on their own, attempt to halt the downward spiral of a deflating economy primarily through fiscal and monetary policy, although a number of other strategies also tend to be added to the fight. Fiscal policy uses revenue and expenditure activity to attempt revival of a country's economy. By raising or lowering taxes, or by providing certain tax benefits to targeted parts of the economy, the government may be able to maintain consumption and/or channel investment in a particular direction. Or sometimes the government will just spend directly. The idea is for the government to take over the burden of the economy for the portion that has fallen. But whatever action is taken must be funded. And without increasing productivity and creating wealth, it becomes a zero-sum game. It's redistribution, moving money from one pocket to another. And at some point, the funding must be repaid.

Fiscal policy, by way of direct funding, has often been undertaken through general maintenance programs – huge projects for enhancing and repairing the country's infrastructure, for instance. Highway construction or improving the electrical grid or building bridges, etc. Naturally, these projects require more debt. Infrastructure of a society must be constantly maintained and expanded. When other parts of the economy are failing, it makes perfect sense to focus on public projects that would be required sometime in the future anyway. Franklin D. Roosevelt used his New Deal strategy as an attempt to pull the U.S. out of the Great Depression with massive infrastructure projects. From 1933 to 1936, the government instituted a huge fiscal stimulus, which temporarily relieved the symptoms of the diseased economy. Other countries followed suit. Hitler embarked on a massive military buildup as well as his ambitious autobahn project, reaching something close to full employment by 1936. That same year, opposition in the U.S. to further government stimulus programs financed with ever-increasing debt finally brought a halt to further stimulus. It was considered no longer necessary. The New Deal was dead. The economy had bounced back. Or so it seemed. In reality, the bump in the economy was due almost entirely to the stimulus. The economy had become dependent upon it (not unlike today's economy), and when it was pulled in 1937 at the same time other countries pulled their stimulus programs, the result was global recession, with consequences in Germany that would help motivate Hitler to take control of Austria and the Sudetenland, and, one year later, to invade Poland.

In addition to fiscal policy there is monetary policy, a means by which to control the supply of a country's money, typically by trying to target a particular interest rate, thereby making it more, or less, attractive to borrow. Monetary policy is generally controlled by a country's central bank. When people borrow, the money supply increases, encouraging consumption, investment, and asset purchases. Conversely, when the money supply contracts, people are paying down debt (or defaulting), and consumption, investment, and asset purchases recede. During a recession or depression, the money supply contracts of its own accord. Central banks, through lessons learned in the past, put forth tremendous effort toward increasing the money supply against the prevailing, naturally contracting forces. But in a global meltdown, it can be like building a dike in front of a tsunami. And ultimately any measure to increase the money supply must, by definition, increase debt.

Over the last few decades, when little else was working, central banks came up with a new monetary tool: quantitative easing (QE). QE is just another approach to increase the money supply. By now it should be clear that the money supply can only be increased by debt. But QE is an innovative new tool used by central banks that keeps the debt "off the books" of the economy. A central bank might institute QE if increasing the money supply through interest rate policy has hit its limit (rates are bounded by zero on the downside, after all). QE is a strategy by which the central bank buys up financial assets from commercial banks (as distinguished from the more conventional buying and selling of government bonds) to try to inject more dollars into the economy's money supply. The U.S. Federal Reserve has accomplished this by crediting the banks' accounts at the Fed with reserves, kind of like putting the purchases of the assets on some kind of massive Fed credit card for which the balance is owed to itself. QE is a lot like the old and sometimes disastrous practice of printing extra money during times of financial difficulties.

The effectiveness of QE has been hotly debated. There is no doubt that QE causes a rise in asset prices and currency devaluation while the strategy is in place. This can boost confidence in the short term. When the housing and stock markets are going up, there's obviously a brighter outlook than when those markets are falling. But what happens when the program stops? Are the assets artificially inflated above their true productive values? And of course the banks are free to do with the money as they see fit, which might include just holding onto it or buying the same assets that the Fed is buying (riding the trend on the upward price pressure caused by the Fed's buying spree) rather than lending it out, thereby counteracting the effectiveness. For all the supposed benefits of QE, there is no conclusive evidence that it has any effect on the development of new productivity. It would seem, instead, that the consequences of QE tend to foster unsustainable asset inflation, encourage further – possibly excessive – consumption, and forestall the reconciliation of the excessive debt problem.

If quantitative easing works even on a temporary basis, it is because of the relative strength of the nation's currency. QE can be a workable strategy for the U.S., for example, because of the relative strength of the dollar. Other nations don't have this advantage. Japan has used QE, but only because of their relatively high savings rate. They can draw against their savings to finance it. In the case of the United States, QE is financed by the unwavering full faith and credit of the U.S. government. But this can be problematic from a global political point of view. Resentment festers around the world when the standard of living in other countries goes down due to a global financial crisis, but the standard of living in the United States remains unscathed, maintained by a continuing dependence on debt, financed in part by QE's intended effect of weakening the dollar – the world's reserve currency.

As mentioned, besides fiscal and monetary policies, there are other actions a government might take to help confront the crisis. On a political level, these may often seem unrelated to the economic battle. Setting up protective trade policies, restricting or encouraging foreign immigration, forcing the use of underutilized assets, encouraging foreign investment, changing the legal and regulatory environment, manipulating currency, or thwarting economic competitors are all examples of policies that might be presented in political rather than economic terms. In reality, however, these actions are frequently calculated to either bring in resources from outside the economy or redistribute underutilized domestic wealth. It's almost always about the economy.

If wealth cannot be created or appropriated, and further borrowing is exhausted, some countries will try to relieve their debt burden by default or through devaluing their currency and inflating their way out of the debt. The payback, if there is one, becomes less onerous with currency that is worth less. These approaches, however, come with significant consequences in world standing, limiting a country's future borrowing and potentially creating severe price inflation for the domestic economy. There is no free lunch.

It's clear that governments can do various things to try to alleviate pain during the lag in productivity. Ironically, the repairs offered by the government, calculated to delay the effects of the crisis until productivity catches up, often have the effect of delaying the very productivity that's being anticipated. The postponement of the pain means a postponement of incentive. Necessity is the mother of invention, but what happens when the government, trying (in its cumbersome way) to do the right thing, takes away necessity?

Too, hanging on to the promise of some significant uptick in productivity is made more insufferable in an economy that is predominantly service oriented. Efficiencies in manufacturing don't really have a counterpart in the world of service. Service-dominated economies primarily grow only through increased services, which are limited by money supply (income and debt) and the population of the economy. There are only so many haircuts or car washes required in any given population in any given time period. And to what end do these services further the economy? Manufacturing-dominated economies, in contrast, grow through production efficiencies and the redeployment of slack created by those efficiencies. Unfortunately, many Western economies (especially the U.S.) have shifted a vast majority of their manufacturing prowess overseas and their economies are now dependent on the drivers of service-based economies.

In a global crisis, with countries around the world feeling the effects, fiscal, monetary, and other (political) actions are often taken by many different governments at once, with counterproductive results. It becomes a zero-sum game where some countries win and others lose but the global net effect remains virtually unchanged. The steps one country's government takes might adversely affect another country, often by negating the second country's own policy actions. Trying to make exports more attractive by increasing the money supply, for instance, doesn't help if foreign money supplies are being increased at the same time. Trade protectionist policies aren't very helpful if every country around the world is instituting them. If the U.S. monetizes its oil resources, serious ramifications will likely result elsewhere, chiefly in the Middle East. But in a crisis, it's not easy for political leaders being pressured at home to keep their eyes on the results of their actions elsewhere in the world. There is a tendency to withdraw in a crisis, to pull back and hunker down. In good economic times, the world is open and connected. In a global crisis, that connectivity begins to break apart as countries retreat unto themselves and institute, with little concern for worldwide implications, policies designed to help their own citizenry. An already tense atmosphere from the economic crisis becomes more tense with geopolitical stress.

With all that government can do to try to alleviate the pain of a financial crisis, a government cannot do the one thing necessary to cure a diseased economy: create wealth. Only increased productivity can do this. But in times of global systemic crisis, the potential for increased productivity is held back, restricted by the current structure of the world's economic environment. Time, space, or matter must be made more efficient through creativity and technological innovation. And the resulting slack must be redeployed into further productive endeavor.

When new wealth creation cannot be generated and the world's debt continues to mount, leading to further global financial inequality and divisiveness, what – specifically – happens next? Volatility increases around the globe and begins to manifest itself in certain ways and certain places, ways and places that represent open wounds. The impediments to progress start to become clearly visible, impediments that create dangerous vulnerabilities. A king relying on taxation in the dying order of Absolutism. Slavery in the dying order of Self-Determination. Fascism and imperialism in the dying age of Nationalism. These impediments become anachronistic. And lethal.

For the world to move on economically, the impediments need to be resolved, and their resolutions never come peacefully. What are the impediments of our age? What and where, are today's lethal vulnerabilities? If the world goes to war, against what will it fight? And what will it defend?

CHAPTER FOURTEEN

Oil

Formula for success: rise early, work hard, strike oil.
J. PAUL GETTY

When new world orders arise, they have a cleansing effect, ridding the globe of that which has been impeding humankind's next big leap forward. Dying world orders harbor such impediments. The impediments are, in fact, what leads to the dying. In the mid-1770s, humankind found itself in a position where it could make no significant advance in a world order that was based upon Absolutism. Absolutism spawned imperialism and exploitative mercantilism, bringing great wealth to the monarchs, but eventually becoming outdated. In time, these structures became the vulnerabilities of the age, leading to the eventual demise of Absolutism. In the mid-1800s, at a time when strong, federal nations were required to amass the resources and means of the Industrial Revolution, humankind found itself encumbered by a world order based on small, decentralized societies and governments, leaden with outdated systems like slavery that inhibited further industrialization. In the early part of the twentieth century, humankind was stifled by old-order empires that became pitted against one another, leading to the fervor of nationalism in the extreme, escalated ultimately into the likes of fascism, imperialism, and communism. In each case, the power and the wealth that evolved under the economics of the old order (more so than ideology alone, as is commonly supposed) weighed down the progress of the world once the old system began its slide into dysfunction.

Each time, what the new world order did was wipe the slate clean. The impediments were removed. As this era's world order breathes its last, the impediments that are stifling us now must be examined. These are the barriers that must be removed in order for dramatic human advancement to begin again, the obstructions that a new world order will eliminate.

The elimination will come by fire, as it must. The impediments will not die easily. Indeed it is the impediments that will provide the very foundation of war, as the tethers of colonialism and slavery and extreme nationalism provided the grounds for the global conflicts of prior world orders. It must be remembered that the bulk of the world's power rests with those whose interest is the status quo. Those who hold sway over the current world order have amassed wealth and influence from it. They will be reluctant to let it go and they will have the wherewithal to maintain the order far beyond its once useful and efficient life.

In addition to those who will hold to the status quo, there will be those who may see that change is necessary but who will nevertheless attempt to mitigate its intensity and potential violence through deferment and compromise. But when there is systemic failure, there are no good options to choose from so long as one is working from within the system itself. If the objective is to prolong the life of a dying system, one can only hope to pick the least bad available option. It's tossing deck chairs off the *Titanic.* Recall the ineffective actions governments take in their attempts to resolve dying economies, postponing the inevitable for as long as they can. This shows up with geopolitical matters as well.

An especially stark example from history is the Munich Agreement. British Prime Minister Neville Chamberlain, witnessing Germany's rise to power, felt as though the rise could be contained. Believing Hitler's intentions to be limited, he traveled to Munich in September of 1938 and signed the agreement that would allow Nazi Germany to annex portions of neighboring Czechoslovakia. Chamberlain returned to London and proclaimed "peace for our time." In Chamberlain's mind, the Munich Agreement was the least bad option, reflecting the desperate desire of Germany's competing powers to maintain the status quo at whatever the cost. Others recognized the futility. The Munich Agreement was an act of appeasement that, rather than placate Hitler, would serve to further embolden him. "England," Churchill said, "has been offered a choice between war and shame. She has chosen shame, and will get war." Six months later, Germany would take the remainder of Czechoslovakia. Six months after that, Germany would invade Poland, touching off World War II.

Keeping the counter forces of status quo and change in mind, this chapter and the two that follow will consider the impediments of today's world. These are the last remnants of the Superpower world order that represent the vulnerabilities of *our* age. These will be the grounds for war. And each must be – will be – resolved in the new world order.

The place to start is to consider the very thing that keeps humankind moving in the first place, an unresolved matter the vulnerability of which is magnified by its importance: the world's source of energy. Energy makes light, energy creates goods, energy provides transportation, and energy produces and delivers food – the body's energy. Energy is nothing less than life. More specifically, in our day and age, the world lives on oil or at least energy that is derived from so-called fossil fuels – petroleum, coal, and natural gas. Over 80% of the world's energy is from these fuels, with roughly 15% from renewable energy (e.g., wind, solar, geothermal, hydropower) and the remaining from nuclear.

Why is so much energy derived from oil? Because oil has been and is today the cheapest and most efficient source of energy by far. Moreover, the world has become dependent upon it. From its extraction and refinement to its distribution and use, the world's infrastructure has been built around it. Trillions of dollars have been invested in this infrastructure. Economies of scale exist that alternative energy sources cannot possibly compete with. We haven't yet learned to efficiently produce, store, and transport other forms of energy on anywhere near the same scale. Renewables might work at their source but need to go through conversions to be transportable and are stored inefficiently in batteries and other mediums. Oil – fossil fuels in general – can be transported and stored and held in huge reserves.

And oil is plentiful. Proven oil reserves have increased by over 50% in the past decade alone. The United States has increased production, threatening to unseat Russia and Saudi Arabia as top oil producers. Brazil and China and Japan have also increased production. Iran is coming back on line. Oil-fields have been exploited in Africa. Canada has immense reserves. Moreover, demand has slowed due to gains in efficiency, as well as by small inroads made by alternative energy sources. And perhaps most importantly by the fact that productivity, fueled at every level to some extent by oil, is off. Any increase in oil consumption has more or less been as a function of the increase in population. Supply is high and there's no reason to think this will change any time soon.

There are, of course, ecological reasons to turn away from fossil fuels, but it's hard to imagine a swift and smooth transition. Even if someone came up with an amazing new source of energy – one that's ecologically friendlier, even cheaper, the switch would take years and years. It's like when you buy a new car and the next year another model comes out. It's better. It's got more bells and whistles. Maybe it gets better gas mileage and has more trunk space and a sunroof. Maybe it's even less expensive. Do you run out and buy it? If you're like most people, you're going to keep the car you just bought, running it into the ground before you invest in the latest model. All of which is to say that oil now holds a formidable position in the global economy and, indeed, society. It will not be knocked off its throne anytime soon without dramatic action – the kind of action that changes world orders.

Oil's abundance from the variety of relatively new production sources versus an increase in consumption that can only be measured incrementally (due to more efficient use, economic stagnation, and the forces behind alternative energies), presents a huge problem for the world and especially for countries whose economies have been largely dependent on oil production. The Middle East, of course, is heavily concentrated with countries that are especially dependent on oil for their livelihood. Approximately 50% of GDP and more than 75% of all exports for Saudi Arabia, United Arab Emirates, Qatar, Kuwait, Iraq, and Iran are dependent on oil. The increased supply has created havoc for these countries. In June of 2008, the price of crude oil was over $140 per barrel. In 2014, the price plummeted to approximately $40 and it has yet to recover to anywhere near the familiar benchmark price of $100 per barrel. And there is no reason to believe the price will rise any time in the foreseeable future. Even if the price does rise, that would only incentivize more production from non-Middle East sources, again forcing downward pressure on price. As long as supply is high relative to demand (and there is nothing right now that can change this), a cap on pricing is unavoidable. So too is the further economic demise of the oil-dependent Middle East region. And the Middle East isn't the only area suffering from the glut of oil. At least 25% of Russia's economy depends on oil and natural gas. Fossil fuels account for half of all its exports. For these countries – the established, old-guard oil-producing countries – the realities of supply and demand are causing significant economic damage.

Of course when demand goes down for these old-guard producers, they can attempt strategies in the hopes of protecting their declining incomes. They can move to drop the price of oil even further, positioning themselves better in the marketplace in the hopes of gaining a greater share of oil sold. They can do this by overproducing, keeping supply high thus keeping the pricing low. The Middle East and Russia and other old-guard countries dependent on oil production can do this and still make a profit. Their costs are low relative to other countries because their oil fields are in operation, their oil is easier to get at, and their drills are in place. They're already set up. For other, up-and-coming oil producers with higher cost structures, a drop in price below their cost is a hard pill to swallow. For countries like the U.S. that rely on higher cost production such as fracking or offshore oil rigs or expensive transport, the drop in price could mean a sudden barricade to any newfound energy independence and wealth-creation strategy.

The real problem for the established oil-producing countries is that reducing their price of oil, although perhaps effective in maintaining or increasing their level of exports, will still put their respective economies under duress. It's a strategy at odds with their self-interests. This contradiction exists because of the portion of their economies devoted to oil and the enormous amount of additional market share that would have to be obtained to offset the drop in price. If all you sell is oil, a 10% decrease in price means a 10% decrease in your GDP, unless it is offset by a much greater than 10% increase in sales (considering profit margin and costs of production). That's a big decrease. If the U.S. GDP fell 10%, the nation would be in a depression.

And so the countries are damned if they do and damned if they don't. They can maintain their level of oil production and keep their prices higher, but this risks losing business to the newly-competing oil-producing countries which might be able to sell their oil at similar pricing. The other choice is to overproduce and increase the supply of oil and watch as the pricing falls due to the increased supply. So, you either sell less or you sell at a reduced price. Either way, your profits get slashed.

Saudi Arabia has chosen to continue to overproduce. Their goal is to outlast the new producers, outlast the rise in alternatives, and outlast the continued technological efficiencies of oil's usage. But the strategy is flawed. The Saudis, clinging to a world system that is rapidly becoming dangerously outdated, cannot outlast the direction the world is heading. Regrettably for the Saudis, the current ruling power has no other choice. Even if it was decided to go a different route, the country would still have to go through tremendous economic upheaval, most likely combined with a tumultuous shift in power.

Meanwhile, to maintain their economy and the level of their government spending, the Saudis are burning through their foreign currency reserves, turning to debt, and encouraging foreign investment. Recently, in an effort to infuse their economy with more money, they've even opened their stock market to foreign investors, something they'd never considered before. All of these strategies point to the economic bind the country finds itself in as a result of the global oil glut, an irreversible economic bind for as long as the status quo is maintained.

Another potential approach that the vulnerable oil-producing countries must be considering is the physical restriction of the oil distribution of the competing countries. The distribution network forged by the established world order, relied upon by the old-guard and once working quite nicely, could be put at risk. In the face of changing allegiances, competing economic motivations, and geopolitical loggerheads, Russia or the Middle East oil producers could wield dominance over existing modes of oil transport (shipping or pipeline) or attempt to thwart new ones. They could exert political pressures, economic influence, covert or overt involvement, or even military aggression disguised as defensive in nature and passed off as an attempt to protect one's own interests and citizenry (think Ukraine). If they can find ways to make it harder for the competing countries to take their oil to the world market, they can be sure to get their oil there first. Yet another source of dissonance to the rhythm of the ailing world order.

A common (perhaps naive) question is often asked by the West: Given the potential difficulties, why don't countries whose economies are largely dependent on oil just diversify? Because oil is how the countries – and more to the point, the leadership of the countries – made their wealth in the first place. It's not something they're keen on giving up. It's what they know. And introducing something new into the economic equation means the potential for having to introduce new, perhaps foreign elements of influence. An example might be foreign investment capital. That means having to share the wealth. And power.

The very structure of these countries, further discussed in the next chapter, has come from oil, and structural change does not come easily. Of course the structure has, in turn, become self-fulfilling. Diversification at this point would mean great change and great change would result in political instability. And money in the form of investment capital has an unsurprising tendency to stay away from environments where the rule of law is inconsistent and leadership is shaky. Saudi Arabia, for example, can attempt to attract outside investors, but will the world invest in a nation at risk for devolving into turmoil? Even if they wanted to diversify, these countries have long ago forfeited their chance at it. They've painted themselves into the proverbial corner. With oil. They're stuck with the structure they have. And, as with any incumbent power, they will exert no small effort to maintain the status quo.

The question is whether they can hold it in the long run. The budding volatility may well lead (is leading now) to instability everywhere because of the importance of oil to the rest of the world. In these times of lower wealth creation and productivity, the "pie" of oil is being sliced into smaller and smaller pieces. We might not notice this in the West. But for the established oil-producing countries, the effect is felt deeply. As we have seen, the hallmark of flat-lining productivity is financial inequality, and this is what is now being felt most keenly in the countries of the world that are the most dependent on oil production. This tension is contributing to incidents such as those witnessed with the Arab Spring and the recent events in Ukraine. The old-guard, oil-producing countries represent a huge unresolved vulnerability in this, the post-Superpower world order period of history.

The U.S. and the rest of the world can stay out of the way, of course, but problems in oil-producing countries mean a potential decrease in oil supply, especially at the pricing we're used to seeing from those sources. What if suddenly the political circumstances of those regions – maybe civil war, for example – meant that those regions were no longer viable sources of oil for the rest of the world?

There is something further to consider: the U.S. Energy Information Administration has identified seven significant oil "chokepoints" – channels within maritime routes that are widely used but so narrow that, in places, the size of the ships that can navigate them are restricted. Several are located in regions that are geopolitical hotspots. The Strait of Hormuz, for example, located between Oman and Iran, connects the Persian Gulf with the Gulf of Oman and the Arabian Sea. At one point it's no wider than twenty-one nautical miles. Seventeen million barrels of oil a day flow through the Strait of Hormuz. That's almost the entire U.S. daily consumption. The Suez Canal, linking the Red Sea and Gulf of Suez with the Mediterranean is another such chokepoint. So is the Strait of Malacca, running between the Indian Ocean to the South China Sea and the Pacific Ocean. Every day, fifteen million barrels of oil are moved through this strait which at one point is less than two miles wide. The Bab-el-Mandeb (Mandab Strait) situated between the Arabian Peninsula and the Horn of Africa connects the Red Sea to the Gulf of Aden for access to the Indian Ocean. Its narrowest point is only eighteen miles wide. If at any time, any of these chokepoints fall into the hands of terrorists or a rogue state or is otherwise disrupted by hostilities or outright war, the flow of the world's energy supply would be severely crippled, causing rising energy prices the likes of which would devastate an already-ailing global economy. Such an incident would force involvement in the shorter term and possibly an independent energy platform in the longer term.

Again, any move away from Middle Eastern oil would be particularly problematic for the old-guard, oil-producing countries. They're happy with their current customer base. For its part, the U.S. has been happy with the arrangement, too. People wonder why the United States has seemingly had no energy policy in place as an alternative to its dependence on the Middle East without realizing that our dependence on the Middle East *has* been our energy policy. It has been easier and cheaper to go to the countries whose main business is oil. This only made sense. There was no smarter choice. Over the long run, for better or worse, the U.S. determined that keeping a foothold in the Middle East was the best, cheapest, and most efficient means of securing oil (not that that policy has exactly come trouble-free.) Now, American policy makers are suggesting that this strategy may no longer be viable.

But is independence of Middle East oil practical at this point? The U.S., consuming nineteen million barrels of oil *per day* is by far the world's biggest oil consumer. The European Union consumes close to fourteen million barrels per day. Japan, close to five million. India and Canada represent another six million. What if the U.S. and its allies greatly reduced their consumption of oil from the Middle East and Russia? Is such an action feasible? Is it desirable? In such a case, the old-guard oil countries could become economic disaster zones, tinderboxes for something catastrophic. Can the rest of the world simply walk away? Nature, and history, abhors a vacuum. The U.S. would be involved because the entire world would feel the repercussions.

What's more likely, of course, especially in light of the relative expense of alternative energies, is for the U.S. and its allies to remain involved, to attempt to avert the potential catastrophe, to keep the flow of oil moving (and affordable). But where does this involvement lead and what shape will it take?

It's easy to take energy for granted. Energy is ubiquitous. It's in everything you touch. But what happens if the established global energy platform suddenly becomes threatened by the volatility of a changing world order in the throes of a productivity stagnation marked by significant economic instability and financial inequality? What happens when the decreasing value of such a universal commodity creates a frantic grab for whatever market share can be acquired? And at whatever cost is deemed acceptable by an oil-producing country led by a desperate government? Much is up in the air. There are uncertainties in the distribution of oil and the relationships of nations that buy and sell it, which, of course, includes every nation in the world. There is a tremendous push for alternative forms of energy. Germany, in fact, is now close to getting 30% of its energy from renewable resources. Other European countries are following suit. The U.S. will move inevitably in that direction. Of course it will take time. But the unpredictability of the energy markets is palpable and the threat to the old-guard, oil-producing countries is real. And imminent. There are impediments that must be resolved. Barriers that are holding the world back from its next leap forward, even as old-order paradigms are being clung to. But what we know from history is this: resolution will take place. It always does.

CHAPTER FIFTEEN

The Middle East

It's not a democracy here, it's the Middle East.
SILVAN SHALOM

*The Middle East has the highest unemployment percentage
of any region in the world, we have the largest youth
cohort of history coming into the market place... that
frustration does translate into the political sphere when
people are hungry and without jobs.*
ABDALLAH II, KING OF JORDAN

Tarek al-Tayeb Mohamed Bouazizi sold produce out of
a cart in a small town in Tunisia. He did his best to provide
for his family, but the local government was corrupt and
Bouazizi was always being harassed, even publicly humiliated,
by government officials in efforts to extort money from him.
His little cart was often confiscated with various claims about
him not having this or that vending license. The harassment
was not uncommon in the town (indeed throughout the
country), and although bribes often worked for other vendors,

Bouazizi didn't have the money to bribe the officials. Struggling, his pride hurt, his prospects dim, Bouazizi stood outside the governor's office on the 17th of December, 2010, and yelled, "How do you expect me to make a living?" Then he doused himself with gasoline.

With the lighting of a single match, Bouazizi ignited the Arab Spring.

After Bouazizi's self-immolation, protests sprang up around Tunisia and elsewhere. It seems Bouazizi wasn't the only one feeling oppressed by the governments of the Middle East nations. His act resonated with others (several even copied it), and demonstrations began that became increasingly angry and violent. People protested corruption, high unemployment, poor living conditions, and repression of free speech. Tunisia's president, in power since 1987, was forced out within two weeks of Bouazizi's death.

In time, the rulers of Egypt, Libya, and Yemen would also be ousted. There would be major revolts in Iraq, Kuwait, and Jordan. Syria would devolve into civil war. Protests would take place in Bahrain, Morocco, Algeria, Oman, Sudan, Mauritania, and Saudi Arabia. Hardly a Middle East nation would be left untouched by the dissension of the people of the Arab world. If energy represents an unresolved vulnerability, the world's major source of it represents an even bigger one. The Middle East is the stumbling block of the age – the world's anchor.

It's difficult to imagine there was a time when order in the Middle East was the rule and not the exception. Beginning in the Middle Ages and until World War I, a lot of today's Middle East was ruled by the Ottomans. A self-proclaimed caliphate – a genuine form of Islamic government – the Ottoman Empire was nevertheless more of an old world regime, with monarchs and kingdoms. As the hegemonic force in the region, it controlled or strongly influenced much of the modern-day nations of Turkey, Syria, Jordan, Saudi Arabia, and Egypt. The only other major competitor in the Middle East was Persia, and the two empires would engage in war several times. Sultans and shahs would come and go, and power and territory would swing back and forth depending on the results of the latest war. But for the most part, at least within each empire, there was stability. The conflicts between the empires remained between them. The outside world went about its business, generally unaffected.

The major difference between the Ottoman and the Persian regions was religious in nature and a distinct hatred came about between the two domains and their respective takes on Islam. After Mohammad's death in the year 632, a split took place in the fledgling Muslim world. The Sunnis believed Mohammad's rightful successor was his father-in-law. The Shias believed that Mohammad had divinely ordained his cousin. The two sides soon developed significant differences in their religion's texts and practices. The Ottoman Empire was a Sunni state, the Persian was Shia, and the split became violent, fueling war. More than thirteen hundred years later, the division remains unresolved, with the Sunnis still at violent odds with the Shias.

With the two main powers established, religious rule would become the region's means of governance from the time of the split. But with those two authorities in control, everyone moved lockstep. You had a scattering of each group in each domain, but it was clear who was calling the respective shots. For the most part, even Jews and Christians were able to live within the domains in relative peace.

So it was for hundreds of years. But then things became complicated, and dangerous, when the empires began to fold. Both empires lost ground to Europe's industrial advancement in the nineteenth century creating the chance for Europe and Russia to expand their interests at the expense of the Ottomans. Once again, the Western world saw opportunity to reclaim access to the Christian Holy Land and, along with it, control of the region's resources and strategic trade routes. The immediate result was the Crimean War, marking the West's new insertion into the affairs of the Middle East. Over the next 150 years, the West would continue to strengthen its foothold in the Middle East every time there was major conflict.

The Crimean War left the Ottoman Empire intact during the next half- century, but ultimately compelled it to seek alignment with the (losing) German and Austrian Empires during the First World War. And thus that war would mark the end of the Ottomans. The modern Arab world was created out of the broken pieces of World War I, with little regard for religious and cultural differences. The Arabs, who had been oppressed by the Ottoman reign, had helped the British defeat the Ottomans during the war on the promise of pan-Arab sovereignty in the region of modern day Syria, Iraq, Jordan, Lebanon, and Saudi Arabia. In the aftermath of the war, however, the promise went unfulfilled. The region was divided into several new nations with geography and power decided by the European victors. France took mandates over Syria and Lebanon. Great Britain took mandates over Iraq, Jordan, and Palestine, and did not stop there.

Much of Persia, which became Iran, had been occupied by the British military during the war. The British would eventually withdraw their troops in 1921, but they would return, along with the Soviets, during World War II to secure Iranian oil for the Allied war effort. Again, foreign powers would create political upheaval inside Iran. The Soviets finally left and the British could not afford to stay, but the Americans would fill the void. In 1953, the CIA would be instrumental in an Iranian coup, instituting a Western-friendly monarch. Post-World War II, the new Shah of Iran, along with the King of Saudi Arabia, would become the West's biggest cheerleaders in the region. The stage would now be set for the power struggles within and between the countries of the Arab world that continue to this day.

The effects of these power struggles began to boil over in the 1970s as the Western world became fairly oil-dependent on the Middle East. The West began to exercise more and more influence over the area, threatening to slowly erode the region's theocratic underpinnings and moral beliefs. The outside world, and its twentieth century culture, had moved in. Many in the area responded with Islamic fundamentalism – the so-called Islamic Revival which included the Iranian Revolution in 1979. But the retreat towards fundamentalism had the effect of reawakening the differences between the Sunnis and the Shias. And since the laws of each establish that their religions govern most aspects of their societies, the differences led to political, as well as religious strife. Sectarian conflicts heated up.

Iran would soon be invaded by neighboring Iraq. Worried that Iran's revolution would encourage one in his own country, the path for Saddam Hussein – a Sunni leading a mostly Shia state – would be the Iran-Iraq war. Lasting from 1980 until 1988, the war cost the lives of a million people, soldiers and civilians alike. The uprising Saddam had feared would take place in 1991 following his defeat in the Gulf War. He would brutally repress it. Between 50,000 and 100,000 of Saddam's own citizens (Shia citizens) would be killed.

Today, points of Shia-Sunni conflict can be found in Iraq, Pakistan, Afghanistan, Syria, Egypt, Jordan, Yemen, Bahrain, Lebanon, Saudi Arabia, and to some extent pretty much every other Middle East country. The conflict is characterized by one side's oppression of the other, resulting in protests and election boycotts on the peaceful end of the spectrum; terrorist acts, suicide bombings, and all-out civil war on the other.

Because Middle Eastern countries are essentially theocratic, the sectarian violence will not end any time soon. Islam – in one form or another – will continue to be tangled up in the political affairs of the region's governments until religion and state are separated, much as they eventually were in Europe following the Thirty Years' War in the seventeenth century.

Today, with the Arab Spring, the governments of the Middle East nations are under attack, regardless of whether they are Sunni or Shia. Financial inequality is rampant in the Middle East, an extension of the world's current (record) financial inequality. Conventional wisdom has it that the Arab Spring is about democracy. The people are rising up to break the shackles of totalitarian rule to gain more of a say in how their countries are run and get the rights we in the West take for granted. But it's strange, the timing. These countries have been run as they are for decades upon decades, under theocratic structures with which the respective populations have generally always been on board. Is it just coincidence that riots are breaking out now, at a time when the economies of these countries are in such steep decline? Unemployment is widespread. Poverty is severe. People are starving and corruption is rampant. In truth, it would make little difference if the rulers were ostensibly ordained by Allah or democratically elected by the people. Their regimes would still be threatened.

Of course the volatility of the Middle East isn't limited to Shia-Sunni conflict or economic disaffection. In the late 1800s, a movement to find a homeland for the world's Jews gained steam. Zionism was pressing to counter the effects of the Diaspora, the historical exile of the Jews from their original homeland in modern-day Israel. The Jews had been dispersed throughout the world, but mostly to Europe. During the centuries following the sacking of Jerusalem by the Romans, and the destruction of its Jewish Temple in 70 A.D., a great many more Jews would come to live outside of the Middle East than in. By 1900, for instance, the world's Jewish population stood at approximately 11 million, of which 9 million lived in Europe and 1.5 million in the Americas. Less than a few hundred thousand Jews were living in the Judea.

Europe, meanwhile, was steeped in anti-Semitism, perhaps best exemplified by the Dreyfus Affair. In 1894, Alfred Dreyfus, a French artillery officer of Jewish descent was sentenced to life in prison at the infamous Devil's Island in French Guiana after being wrongfully convicted of spying for the Germans. Two years later, it was revealed that the real spy was another man. Dreyfus was brought back for a retrial, but the belief in his innocence was hardly universal. Those lining up against him weren't shy about voicing their anti-Semitic opinions: Jews could not be trusted. The affair bitterly divided France and revealed the anti-Semitism of the age.

Watching it all unfold was an Austro-Hungarian journalist named Theodor Herzl. Herzl had witnessed growing anti-Jewish sentiment before. By then it had grown rampant. In Russia in May of 1882, the minister of internal affairs Nikolai Ignatyev proposed a set of laws designed to contain the influence of the Jewish population. Known as the May Laws, they were intended to be temporary measures but continued to be strengthened over the subsequent three decades. The laws included quotas on the number of Jews that could be admitted to schools and universities, limited Jewish ownership of real property, and even called for deportations. By 1891, few Jews could be found in Moscow and ultimately more than two million Jews would leave Russia. Very little of Europe seemed hospitable to the Jewish population and Theodor Herzl began envisioning an independent Jewish state. He formed the Zionist Organization in 1897, the objective of which was to create a Jewish homeland in Palestine.

Although Herzl would later claim that the Dreyfus Affair

was hugely inspirational to his movement, historians differ on its importance to him (Dreyfus eventually was exonerated, much to the chagrin of those who thought him guilty no matter the evidence to the contrary). But the Dreyfus Affair, the May Laws, and other examples of severe anti-Semitism must certainly have confirmed, if not influenced, Herzl's thinking: Europe was becoming unsafe for Jews.

Herzl could not have possibly anticipated just how unsafe. The movement for a Jewish state was fast-tracked as World War II came to an end and the world began to discover the horrors of the Holocaust. The world collectively offered restitution in 1948 with the formation of the State of Israel. Herzl's dream came true. Out of the British Mandate for Palestine – a spoil from World War I – was appropriated the new Jewish nation. Palestinians and Jews had been battling each other in a civil war since 1947. Once the State of Israel was declared, the civil war became a state conflict between Israel and several Arab countries, including Syria, Egypt, Iraq, and Jordan, all backing the displaced Palestinians. The new country held its ground, but the war created some 700,000 Palestinian refugees and a dangerous, violent resentment.

In the decades since the formation of the State of Israel, conflicts have been commonplace. But Israel has made peace with many of her Middle Eastern neighbors, including Egypt and Jordan, with cease-fires currently in effect with Syria and Lebanon. Israel has since ceded partial (mostly symbolic) control of pieces of Gaza and the West Bank. These territories provide the points of entry for Israel's major threats today. Gaza is governed primarily by Hamas which also holds strong influence in the West Bank. Hamas is a fundamentalist Islamic Sunni organization classified as a terrorist group by much of the world, though little of the Arab world sees it as such. Hamas is not the only terrorist organization Israel needs to contend with. Based in Lebanon and considered stronger than that country's regular army, Hezbollah is the reigning Shia Islamic fundamentalist group. Hezbollah boasts an arsenal of a hundred thousand large-caliber missiles. It is believed they could fire over six hundred missiles a day at Israel if they so chose. If one imagines, by analogy, the suffering of Londoners during the German bombing of their city in World War II, it is not difficult to understand the anxiety being felt by Israelis today.

The terrorist organizations don't end with Hamas and Hezbollah. Within each faction are other factions, splinter groups often at odds with the larger group, and often believing the group, as a whole, has lost its zeal. We saw it with the Palestine Liberation Organization, regarded at one time as a terrorist group and now enjoying observer status at the United Nations. Its major succeeding faction, Fatah, has also lost some standing with the more hardcore anti-Israeli fundamentalists. The main terrorist organizations, in other words, radical in their own right, often give birth to organizations more radical still. Throughout the Middle East, there are dozens of splintered-off terrorist groups with names like the Furqan Brigade and Al Fajr al Islamia and Katibat Abu Qasim. They are everywhere, threatening both Israel and the world.

The fact is, tensions between the Israelis and those seeking a bona-fide Palestinian homeland are firmly entrenched and it's near impossible to imagine a satisfactory solution for both sides. Hatreds run deep and the lands under dispute are not just any lands. They are the holy lands for both the Israelis and Islamic Palestinians. Muddying the waters even more are huge territorial issues, with Israeli settlements encroaching on the Palestinian West Bank and the Israeli-occupied Golan Heights (formerly part of Syria). What does it mean to possess land in this peculiar little area of the world? The question of who owns what cannot be easily answered. How far back does one go? Land titles go back centuries, to the Ottoman Empire.

For Israel's part, there is simply no incentive to surrender to the idea of a two-state solution. The benefits of doing so do not outweigh the potential "game-ending" event of losing the state which has been paid for with countless Jewish lives. So long as there is volatility in the greater Arab world, Middle East terrorist organizations populating the other countries of the region, and wavering guarantees of Western military support, the idea of the Israelis supporting a Palestinian state as a way towards final peace remains a chimera. The extreme Islamic forces controlling a significant part of the Arab world continue to seek the demise of the Jewish state and an independent Palestine does not mean ultimate peace with the entire Arab world, a world that consists of 22 countries and 422 million people (as contrasted with 6 million Jews in Israel and only some 14 million worldwide). Why would Israel surrender adjacent land that is such a vitally important buffer? How could it be imagined that any Israeli government would permit that to happen? In a very real sense, this is Israel's version of the Cuban Missile Crisis. How the United States responded to dangerous encroachment from the Soviet Union is instructive here. Why would it be assumed that Israel would not respond in like manner? Meanwhile, of course, the Palestinians won't give up. What could it possibly take to settle this highly charged standoff?

Some volatility in a region of the world – even a politically important region like the Middle East – can be tolerated. Some cannot. A prime example of volatility that stands up and becomes noticed by even the most disinterested observer is the kind of volatility that comes complete with a nuclear threat. Iran has a nuclear program, ostensibly in place for the sole purpose of providing energy. But Iran keeps developing uranium and is but a stone's throw from enriching it to weapons grade, notwithstanding the agreement with the United States that it will not do so. Of course under normal circumstances, this development would not stand in the eyes of the global community. But Iran is now intent on opening up both its oil and its economy to the rest of the world – Europe and China in particular. By so doing, Iran will ingratiate itself with a significant portion of the world community, turning any potential protestations of nuclear development into delicate diplomatic matters. At that point, Iran may be too valuable to cross.

But Iran's foray into the world oil market is currently being thwarted by Saudi Arabia's resolve to keep the price of oil low by overproducing. This is creating more tension between two major powers that already have a long history of tension. Saudi Arabia is a Sunni kingdom while Iran is a Shia state. Moreover, modern Iran was founded in anti-Western revolution while Saudi Arabia continues to maintain a close, although strained, working relationship with the West. The resentment is palpable. The GDP per capita in Saudi Arabia is five times more than it is in Iran and Saudi outspends Iran on its military by almost five to one. With the development of nuclear weaponry, Iran could turn the tables, gaining regional superiority for itself as well as for the greater Shia movement (and presenting a lethal threat to the rest of the world).

Pakistan is perhaps just as dangerous. Pakistan, after all, currently has over a hundred nuclear weapons. Pakistan is more or less a Western ally (although in continuous conflict with India) and yet remains a breeding ground for terrorists. It might be remembered that Osama bin Laden was eventually found in Pakistan. It is also where he founded al-Qaeda. Worse still, Pakistan's arsenal is spread about the country in a defensive strategy designed to keep the weapons difficult to find. A few nuclear bombs here, a few there – each group protected by military forces the rest of the world hopes never go rogue. The precarious situation of Pakistan partly explains the U.S.

presence in neighboring Afghanistan, a presence whose time is limited.

Afghanistan, incidentally, provides its own unique challenges. Something very interesting was recently confirmed to be present in Afghanistan: rare earth elements (REEs). Seventeen different chemical elements make up the classification known as REEs, and they're used to manufacture batteries, computers, televisions, and other twenty-first century technologies. They're valuable, in other words. The confirmation that Afghanistan held these elements in its earth was made by the United States Geological Survey under protection of the U.S. military. Estimates of the land's worth range up to one trillion dollars. And there are other valuable minerals: copper and zinc and silver. A Pentagon memo calls Afghanistan the Saudi Arabia of lithium. From the Middle Eastern perspective, it is a significant cause for alarm, more of a reason for the Western world to want to sink its teeth into the area, polluting the region with its decidedly non-Islamic ways.

Perhaps no country best represents the turmoil of the Middle East better than Syria which has become the perfect microcosm of the region. Syria also represents a disturbing portent of things to come. The nation has devolved into civil war, with a death toll surpassing 100,000 and refugees by the millions. Small but violent protests against the Syrian government began in 2011 as part of the Arab Spring, but were quickly quelled. Just as quickly, however, the protests started up again, this time going national and being met with the military force of the Syrian Army. The protesters then armed themselves and a full-scale rebellion ensued. By 2013, the government only controlled roughly half of the country.

Syria's conflict is stoked by the same kind of sectarian impasse as the rest of the region. The government is largely Shia and the rebels are largely Sunni. But the roots of the conflict are largely economic – a nation becoming poorer and breaking into parts as the population chases the country's dwindling resources, the parts falling along sectarian lines. Meanwhile, Hezbollah has joined the Syrian civil war on the Army's side. Iran is providing military support to the Syrian government, along with Russia, a long-time Syrian ally. Russia has a naval installation in Syria, giving it strategic access to the Mediterranean Sea. But Russia has another interest, too. The rebels have been joined by Islamic militants from Chechnya – the same militants that have fought for independence from Russia. The Russians know that Syria can become a breeding ground for Chechnyan terrorists.

And another terrorist group has come to power in Syria. The Islamic State of Iraq and Syria (ISIS) now controls a large part of the country and is making significant inroads in neighboring Iraq. ISIS, a Sunni group, got its start as an offshoot of al-Qaeda but their extreme brutality repulsed even al-Qaeda, which eventually cut ties with the group. ISIS has killed thousands of civilians on its ruthless path through the Middle East, executing any who don't adhere to its strict interpretation of radical Islam.

The genesis of ISIS can be directly linked to the often conflicting evolution of the Saudi state. The conservative Islamic theocracy, because of oil and the world's dependency on it, has been challenged by its dealings with a democratic West that is fundamentally opposed to many of its core beliefs. As a result, the Saudi monarchs have been forced to play a difficult balancing game between the West's oil money and power on the one hand, and support from a domestic populace that is steeped in conservative Sunni beliefs on the other. The latter isn't helped by the fact that most of the oil wealth flows directly to the royal family. The three major involved parties – the West, the Saudi monarchs, and the Saudi people – hold positions of self-interest that are deeply entrenched.

So are the rules of engagement among the three. The West has a need for oil. The Saudi monarchs have a need for wealth and power. The Saudi people have a need for their religious beliefs. Collisions are unavoidable.

The West's unspoken (and little publicized) alliance with the Saudi monarchs goes back as far as 1945, to the deck of the warship *USS Quincy*. Saudi king Ibn Saud met with Franklin Delano Roosevelt aboard ship as it lay at anchor in the Suez Canal. FDR, on his way home from meeting Stalin and Churchill at the Yalta Conference, provided assurances to the House of Saud that its reign would be kept secure by the military muscle of the United States. In return, Saudi Arabia would see to it that oil would flow freely to its new American friends. The U.S.-Saudi alliance has survived decades, through war, peace, and one major oil embargo.

Post-9/11, however, the alliance seems to have outlived much of its usefulness to the West. With Saddam Hussein knocking on Saudi Arabia's door during his invasion of Kuwait in 1991, the U.S. went to war. And then went back again in 2003, removing the threat of Hussein permanently, but also helping to produce new threats with the power vacuums created in Iraq and Afghanistan, and the resentment of an entire region. The chain of events since 9/11 has served not only to strain the American-Saudi alliance, but also to magnify the underlying discord of the Middle East. The formation of ISIS, or a similar group, became a foregone conclusion. For now, ISIS is filling the power vacuum in the region, but should ISIS fall, it will be filled again by another movement. The Middle East is an economically struggling population ready to come together under a charismatic power and prepared to vanquish a perceived threat, a common and resented enemy. What resolution can possibly be conceived of for the region? Legend has it that in ancient times, Gordius, the king of Phrygia, tied his chariot to a pole using a knot so

intricate, nobody could untie it. The Middle East is the proverbial Gordian Knot. And things will become more tangled still.

Here is one final example of the ingrained difficulties of
the region, culled from the Israeli situation. Not long ago, a
visionary project dubbed "the ARC," inspired by the RAND
Corporation, was begun with the purpose of strengthening
the physical infrastructure of the West Bank, providing more
connectivity for the Palestinian population, which is economically disjointed and scattered about the area. The thinking
went that if you could raise the standard of living for the
Palestinians through better infrastructure, peace would follow.
But making the project a reality presented enormous challenges.

The 1993 Oslo Accords created three administrative di-
visions for the West Bank. "A" areas were designated as being
under Palestinian control; "B" areas are controlled by both
Palestinians and Israelis (the former in charge of civil administration, the latter in charge of security); and "C" areas
are under Israeli control. The problem is that one cannot
cross from one "A" area to another without having to cross
through a "C" area. The situation prevents viable transportation for moving people and goods throughout the West Bank,
thus thwarting any plans for a connected infrastructure. For
security reasons, there is no motivation for the Israelis to
want to change this. For the Palestinians' part, there is corruption, with whatever investment money that may come in
being usurped by Hamas to aid in their conflict against Israel,
or ending up in the hands of corrupt government officials
who rather like things just the way they are. Any naiveté one
might have about developing the area's infrastructure is
quickly eliminated when one comes to see that the real problems with the area are deeply structural physically, politically,
and culturally. Like many other good ideas intended to solve
the problems of the Middle East, the ARC project went

nowhere. It simply wasn't possible given the current dilemmas of the region.

The Middle East is fraught with these kinds of structural impediments. The region is a systemic failure, offering only bad choices. Who can even say, at this point, what the least bad choice is? There are those in power who seek to cling to the status quo, even as the status quo shifts violently underneath them. There are those seeking to topple the status quo and will resort to whatever brutal means they feel necessary. It is a tragedy playing out before our eyes. The region could be thriving and prosperous; it holds natural resources beyond oil. It is a region rich in history and culture, encompassing the origins of three great religions. There are beautiful landscapes and warm waters. But there are also agendas in place that will make this impossible. For the present, that is.

In the West, we take note of these agendas when they rear up in the form of terrorism. We've responded with a war on terror. It comes with a cost. The U.S. Department of Homeland Security operates with an annual budget of close to one hundred billion dollars. And this is just the beginning. Military spending in the name of anti-terrorism, and all the other intermingled budget programs, add up to an annual tab that is far and above that number. Are we getting our money's worth? We want one hundred percent success. But history and common sense show that no country can insulate itself completely from the outside world if the outside world is intent on barging in. No doubt we'll continue spending more and more, but nothing less than draining the entire treasury can keep us safe and even that cannot be enough. How far, and for how long, will we be willing – and able – to keep up the war on terror? And how does this war get resolved?

And there is another cost to our war on terror: the slow erosion of our freedoms and our collective peace of mind. To some extent, it could be argued that the terrorists are winning in this regard. The strategy of a terrorist is to weaken the will of the enemy, ultimately forcing a division of the enemy's people, leading to capitulation. Hezbollah, Hamas, al-Qaeda, ISIS – they have all learned this lesson. They can find it in history without having to look back any further than Ho Chi Minh's prosecution of the war in Vietnam.

The Middle East is a boiling cauldron. Clearly, the region cannot continue as it is and neither can the rest of the world, which is inextricably tied to it. The Shias and the Sunnis. The Israelis and the Palestinians. The haves and have-nots. The region is in constant revolution and its major source of revenue (oil) is at risk from outside sources. For 2014, oil revenues for the Middle East fell below the $1 trillion mark, a psychological milepost in the wrong direction. And there is no other source of revenue besides oil, no significant capital investment on the horizon, and no agreed upon ideas to fix the problems. Even world aid organizations are weary of sending money that falls into the holes of corruption. There are terrorists. There are nuclear weapons.

The world will advance. And as part of that advancement, the resolution of the quandaries that collectively make up the Middle East vulnerability – however terrible to contemplate – will take place. The Gordian knot, so goes the legend, was eventually solved by Alexander the Great. He cut through it with a sword.

CHAPTER SIXTEEN

The Fall of the Rest...
and the Debt of the West

China is a great country with a great culture, populated by fascinating, industrious and talented people.
VLADIMIR PUTIN

Some foreigners with full bellies and nothing better to do engage in finger-pointing at us. First, China does not export revolution; second, it does not export famine and poverty; and third, it does not mess around with you. So what else is there to say?
XI JINPING

In 2004, Greece hosted the summer Olympic Games in Athens, home of the original, ancient Olympics. By all accounts, the 2004 games were a huge success with International Olympic Committee Chairman Jacques Rogge declaring them "unforgettable, dream games." Millions from around the world tuned in and watched the drama of the games unfold.

Greece was in the world's spotlight. Athens never looked better.

In the years leading up to the opening ceremonies, more than eleven billion dollars were spent on infrastructure and Olympic event venues. A new airport and subway system were just a couple of the improvements that made Athenians, and Greeks in general, proud of their hosting effort. More billions were sent to and spent in Greece by international corporations, foreign governments and organizations, and individuals – all with a stake in the world's biggest and most popular event. Additionally, the Greek government secured further billions of debt just to pay the costs to operate the games. Security costs alone were estimated in excess of one billion dollars.

The infusion of cash created jobs and helped tourism. It drove up real estate and other asset prices. The country's economy went on a nice little upswing. When Greece was chosen as host city in 1997, its annual GDP was approximately $130 billion. By 2004, the GDP had increased to $230 billion – but with no corresponding increase in true productivity or value creation (other than the construction of the required infrastructure). The increase was directly attributable to foreign inflows and domestic debt. All for a one-time event. Yes, people made money and lived better. It was the European feel-good story of the year. But then an unfortunate thing happened: the Olympic Games came to an end. The positive effects of increased tourism lingered for a little while, but soon the attention of tourists was diverted elsewhere. Many of the venues fell into disrepair. The economic upswing from the infusion of cash reversed. The bills came due. The end result? An entire country in economic crisis. Greece's economic success could not be sustained, and neither could its debt.

That Greece's economic problems can be pinned specifically to the 2004 Olympics probably overstates the impact of the games. But the spending spree certainly didn't help and it's reasonable to ask if there is a lesson in all of this, maybe something that can tell us more about the current situation with a few other nations receiving recent infusions of cash, notably Brazil, Russia, India, and China – the so-called BRIC countries. These are the powers on the rise, so goes the thinking. It's not the U.S. anymore. It's the *rest* of the world, embodied by these countries. The story of today's global economy is what's become commonly known as the "Rise of the Rest," coined from Fareed Zakaria's popular book *The Post-American World and the Rise of the Rest.*

This story has it that a new paradigm came into existence with the fall of the Soviet Union. The world turned to democracy and capitalism. Markets were now free. People were now free. And everybody could benefit. Sure, a big chunk might be taken out of the U.S. share of the global economy, but that would be beneficial in the long run. The marketplace was now bigger. There were more consumers. The structure of the world was changing for the better.

In reality, what was happening was that other countries were rising because the dying world order was creating a period of slower wealth creation. As will be recalled from Chapter 12, the West, chiefly the U.S., was in need of lower-cost alternatives in both service and manufacturing to keep the standard of living where it had been. Financed by debt, huge infusions of cash (proceeds from the debt) were directed towards the "Rest," propping up their economies to levels they hadn't seen before.

The BRIC countries provide the best examples of this rise with China, India, and Russia providing perhaps the best summary of it, each having risen by slightly different means. Considering their respective climbs in quantitative terms is revealing. Employing a comparable GDP measurement of purchasing power parity and using U.S. dollars, it can be seen that China's economy has risen from an estimated $5 trillion in 2000 to over $17 trillion today, more than a threefold increase. The surge has come on exports as China has become the low-cost manufacturer to the West. The country is, in fact, the largest exporter in the world now and has an economy roughly equal in size to the U.S. economy.

Changes in China have been nothing less than stunning. Growth within the country has been massive. Cities have swollen as the population has moved from rural areas to cities to meet the manufacturing needs of the world. Over 50% of the population now lives in urban areas, compared to 26% before the fall of the Soviet Union.

India achieved its growth not by exporting manufactured goods, but by exporting services, primarily in the technology sector. Like China, India became a low-cost provider to a world in need of cost-cutting measures. Too, India was the beneficiary of enormous foreign capital investment. More stable than the other BRIC countries, with an established legal system dating back to its days as a part of the British Empire, India became an attractive place to put money. India's GDP has risen from $1.8 trillion in 2000 to $7 trillion in 2014 – another threefold increase in less than fifteen years.

Russia's economy has grown dramatically, as well – from approximately $1 trillion in 2000 to over $3.5 trillion in 2014 – another tripling in less than 15 years. For Russia, the economic growth was sourced in the exportation of commodities – particularly fossil fuels. It's not that these commodities were unavailable for sale during the days of the Soviet Union; rather, it's that the Soviet Union's trading partners were limited in number. When the Cold War ended, Russia's market expanded. As the old nation was imploding economically, it became imperative for the new nation to open itself up to the world. This was seen by many as a wonderful new democratic model. Russia was now all about open markets and freedom. The facts are less romantic. There was no Thomas Jefferson moment in any of this; this was a country seeking a way back from the dead, forced into capitalism (against the very grain of its culture) as a way to survive. After a period of fits and starts (and significant corruption), it finally found its way.

And all of this was happening while the U.S. – one of the most productive countries – experienced "growth" of less than double its GDP from 2000 to 2014. In each case, and in the case of other countries rising in economic power, the impetus was their ability to supply the world with lower costs. Nothing more. Significant value-added productivity was not being created in China, India, or Russia. No new technologies, no exciting innovations. Cheap labor, cheap services, cheaper commodities – this is what was offered and this was what was consumed unreservedly by the West as a means by which to keep the economic engine of the 1990s humming. And as discussed earlier, a lot of the growth was a direct result of increasing debt and the money supply, increases which continue still. This is the new paradigm – the so-called Rise of the Rest. The rise is, in fact, being financed by borrowed money, which means, of course, borrowed time.

The "Rest" are enjoying the fruits of money being infused into their economies, much like Greece enjoyed the fruits of capital up until the Olympic Games ended. But when the world went away, the Greek economy came apart. With the 2008 global recession, Greece was hit especially hard, so much so that eventually, bailouts (by the International Monetary Fund, the European Central Bank, and the European Commission) were necessary, to the tune of 240 billion euros. But the bailouts came with a condition: austerity for the Greek people. Big budget cuts and substantial tax increases. The bailouts were to no avail. Greece continued suffering through a series of recessions while the Greek population chafed against the austerity measures. There is a risk Greece may default on their loans and leave the Eurozone. This would not only create economic problems for the rest of Europe (with global ramifications), it would set a dangerous precedent for other Euro countries risking default.

For China and India and Russia and the rest, the day will also come when the debt (the debt of the West) will come due. The flow of money into these once-rising countries will quickly decelerate. We are beginning to see it even now. The lack of significant wealth creation in the West is creating a dangerous tipping point. Since the new economies are dependent on U.S. and European economic strength, what will happen when that strength diminishes even further? The West does not operate in a vacuum; declining economic growth will have colossal repercussions elsewhere. The world has reached a precarious position.

China's hope is to switch from a producer economy to a consumer one, increasing internal demand to compensate for the slowing external demand. But this is no easy feat. It's not a part of recent Chinese history or culture to spend freely. Even in America it took several generations before consumerism took hold. China could always try to shift its economy from lower value provider (manufacturer of lower value goods) to higher value provider (manufacturer of higher value goods), but in a global economy that is not significantly expanding, this shift would come at the cost of displacement – displacing the countries who are currently manufacturing on the higher end; i.e., the United States or Japan, for instance, creating more global economic turmoil. Moreover, such a shift takes time. And the kind of commitment that comes about only as a result of major upheaval, the kind of shift, in other words, compelled by the stakes of war.

Meanwhile, the urban growth and meteoric rise in manufacturing in China has created problems, not the least of which is stifling pollution in the major cities. Infrastructure is lagging behind, too. China's large amount of uncollectible domestic debt has yet to be reconciled. Property values are inflated. Moreover, China's growth has created a rising dependence on oil. They are expected to soon overtake the United States as the world's biggest oil importer. Competition to supply China will place added pressure on the world's energy platform. And economic growth has not necessarily translated into more economic freedom for the people of China. Businesses are still largely state-controlled, after all. And there is corruption.

In India, the trade deficit is rising and the value of the rupee is falling. Savvy investors are already seeing the writing on the wall and pulling money out of the country. As for Russia, their danger comes, of course, from the increased competition in the energy sector.

Similar problems are befalling the other countries, too. The "Rest" have become vulnerable. When the Superpower world order ended, we cheered. And for good reason. Nobody wants to go back to a cold war. The world was free. But nothing in history happens without unanticipated, unintended consequences. The economic stagnation in the West created markets for low-cost goods and services the "Rest" of the world was happy to provide. And the rest of the world rose, but only on the tide of debt in which the world was awash. But the tide is ebbing.

For the West's part, the massive debt to the Rest is further eroding any hopes for some sort of boost in wealth creation. Even if there would (miraculously somehow) be such a boost, the claim on it would be by the likes of China. Any resulting wealth creation would go unnoticed in the West, certainly by those currently suffering at the hands of the ubiquitous financial inequality.

The sudden rise and surprising fall of a nation is far from unprecedented. In the early 1900s, Argentina was poised to rival the United States in terms of economic power in the Western Hemisphere. By 1913, thanks to soaring levels of agricultural exports, Argentina was the world's tenth wealthiest nation per capita. Significant foreign investment in the country, notably by Great Britain, and cheap labor from a huge influx of immigrants, created the conditions for sudden, massive growth. But within twenty years, the country was economically devastated. Today, in economics classes, the story of Argentina in the first few decades of the twentieth century makes for a popular case study called the Argentine Paradox. The paradox is not so difficult to grasp. World War I forced the British to curtail its investment. Exports dropped. Foreign currency reserves evaporated. Inflation increased. The immigrant population was put out of work. Then came the Great Depression and the final ruin of Argentina's rise, a rise that had been based on foreign investment and the exportation of goods that could be bought elsewhere. The fall of Argentina was as swift as her rise.

There is another lesson in the Argentina Paradox, namely, what came after the fall. The new middle class, falling rapidly backwards on the economic ladder, revolted. A military coup in 1930 dismantled the country's democratic government. Today, for the Rest, a reconciliation of Western debt will soon be due and it will not be pleasant. In the countries of the Rest, new standards of living are in place, as they were in Argentina. Middle classes have sprung up. So have expectations of continued prosperity. In Russia, the middle class grew from eight million in 2000 to fifty-five million in 2006 and it has grown steadily since. China has experienced a building boom. Perhaps its most ambitious project: a replica of the financial district of Manhattan being constructed on a peninsula southeast of Beijing. It's not a tribute to New York. The goal is to have the new city (Yujiapu) become the largest single financial center in the world. But now, several years into its construction, finished and half-finished skyscrapers sit eerily empty. Nobody is investing and the debt is mounting. The boom is turning into a dangerous bust.

When the bubble bursts throughout the nations of the Rest, their populations will not go backwards quietly. They have come too far. The payment will be steep. The people will look to their respective governments for a solution. Having none and risking revolt, their governments may well do what governments are good at in times of crisis – point towards an outside enemy. This is getting less and less difficult to imagine when one considers recent developments in Ukraine.

It's all reminiscent of pre-World War II Germany. Buried under war debts, a middle class nevertheless developed in the late 1920s in large part as a result of American loans. When the Roaring Twenties ended with the stock market crash in '29, banks began calling those loans in. Germany's economy was overwhelmed. Unemployment rose to 20% in less than two months. Hitler, getting little political traction in the 1920s with his message lamenting the oppression of the Fatherland, could not be ignored in the new decade. By 1932, he was Germany's head of state and Supreme Commander of its armed forces. The new middle class was not going away without a fight.

Should such a state of affairs repeat itself now, it may well be the likes of Russia and China that will regard the West as the oppressive powers. When the influx of Western money abates, the classes of struggling people in these countries, who were lately middle-class, will resent the Western wealth, resentment which may be exploited by the Eastern leaders. The competition for the resources of the dying world order, as well as the competition for the leadership of the new world order, will put the Rest and the West on a collision course. Perhaps they are on one even now.

For China's part, it is interesting to note her ongoing military buildup, the recent pace of which is outstripping every other military in the world. Huge investments have been made in warships, submarines, aircraft carriers, nuclear weapons, and (ominously) long-range missiles. So alarmed has Japan become that its leaders are considering reinterpreting the country's constitutional limits on its own military. The constitution of the country, set up post-World War II, allowed only for self-defense. Now Japan's military role is evolving to allow for the defense of Japan's neighbors and allies.

Those neighbors and allies include Malaysia, Taiwan, and the Philippines. Between China and these countries there are conflicting claims and interests in the South China Sea. There are territorial disputes over shipping lanes, and the potential of crude oil under the waters of the South China Sea makes the area valuable and attractive to competing interests. These are the kinds of conditions that can become exacerbated in a fragile world where economies tumble and the masses are moved to action.

There is, for China, incentive only to expand. It is doing so now, throughout the region and indeed throughout the world, investing heavily in the infrastructure of other countries through its "Silk Road" project aimed at further developing its trade. China now has more than five million of its citizens living outside of the country, working in the interests of their nation. Economically and geopolitically, the country, once relatively isolated from the rest of the world, is becoming more and more enmeshed in it. With China's population representing close to 20% of the world, and having the second leading GDP, anything China does has major global ramifications.

Enemies in global conflict do not always come cloaked in evil. Hitler was an aberration, the result of the extremes reached because World War I did not succeed in putting the old order to rest. But make no mistake: wars are mostly waged for self-interest, not for advancing, or deterring, evil. The unthinkable can happen between former friends (England and the Colonies) and even between brothers (the North and South).

As with the energy vulnerability and the Middle East vulnerability, the "Fall of the Rest" vulnerability will need to be sorted out, too. The unsustainable rise, the standard of living expectations that have been established as the new reality, the by-products of living beyond one's productive value – all are contributing to the volatility of the changing world order. Again we see the battle between dramatic change and a dysfunctional status quo, a state of affairs once more presenting nothing better than a search for the least bad alternative. The U.S., for example, must choose between increasing an unsustainable debt position and hoping for the best, or cutting its standard of living. China must choose between foregoing growth or alienating its trading partners and harming its international power status. Russia must risk economic setback to diversify its economy from the reliance on commodities and oil or risk economic setback by doing nothing. Countries in Europe must decide on the benefits of maintaining the euro at the costs of their own self-interests. Japan must weigh the costs of reasserting itself in Asia rather than withering on a dying vine in the shadow of the Chinese. These are just some of the choices the nations of the world must face and none of them will be undertaken in a vacuum. Each decision, or non-decision as the case may be, will create major shockwaves for the rest of the world.

All of this is to say that as the world order of the Superpowers has lost its effectiveness, many potential global powers have evolved, adding to the instability of the status quo. Will some of these new powers be seated at the table of the next world order? Most certainly. Will they all? Likely not. History has established many precedents in this regard. But one thing is certain: the competition for that seating will be fierce.

The vulnerabilities of today's world collectively represent the systemic collapse of this age's world order. Oil, an integral commodity that fueled the world through the twentieth century and beyond, has created two dependencies – those who use it (all of the world at virtually every stage of production and consumption) and those who sell it. The latter are where the dangers lie. The Middle East has suffered the most from the shifting energy paradigm and where the world's economic malaise has manifested itself most plainly and tragically. China and other nations that rose economically with the end of the Superpower world order (including, eventually, Russia) will fall hard from the pedestals constructed by Western debt. Will Russia in particular attempt to hang on to the old order, invoking its lost status as Superpower? Who will line up with the powers of the status quo? Who will enable the continuation of the failing system? And who will recognize the changing direction and help lead the world to a new order? Most significantly, what kind of an order will it be?

CHAPTER SEVENTEEN

On the Other Side

"Again, you can't connect the dots looking forward; you can only connect them looking backward. So you have to trust that the dots will somehow connect in your future."

STEVE JOBS, STANFORD UNIVERSITY COMMENCEMENT,
JUNE 12, 2005

A family moves into a house. It serves their purposes well. It has the required number of bedrooms and baths, it's in the right location, it's in good physical shape, and it has a nice yard. The family thrives in the house. But over the years, the house begins to lose some of what made it so appealing. The carpet, windows, and kitchen cabinetry become dated. The plumbing begins to show signs of wear and tear and so do the electrical system and the roof. Remodeling and some reconstruction are undertaken and that helps. But some of the problems go beyond mere fashion and structure. In some ways, the house loses its ability to serve its inhabitants because the structure of the family itself has changed. Maybe the kids have moved out and some of the bedrooms are now superfluous. Maybe the yard is now too big for the occupants, who have become older or perhaps are in declining health, to manage effectively. Maybe there has been a divorce. Eventually, the house simply outlives its usefulness. The occupants call a realtor, a "For Sale" sign is posted on the front lawn, and the family moves on.

World orders are the structures that the citizens of the world inhabit. As with the example of the house, they're functional and effective and serve their purpose well, but only for a certain period of time. At some point, the old structure must be replaced as no amount of fixing will suffice.

A world order can be defined as a way in which the power of the world at any given time is configured. This configuration creates a system in which everyone is more or less compelled to operate. A world order is the rulebook. It's the house. It is, in short, the way things simply are. Moreover, the order is ordained by the world as legitimate. Through productivity and wealth generated from the system, the order is bestowed the power to enforce the rulebook. With each new world order, there's a common thread of geopolitical thought that runs essentially unopposed or, if opposed, lacking sufficient counteraction to create a viable threat.

As each world order moves toward the end of its useful life, obstructions to humankind's advancement form because the world order fails to accommodate further human advancement. The status quo, by its very nature, is reluctant to let go because of the loss of power and wealth associated with doing so. And it never accepts that the power and wealth will eventually be lost anyway. Conflict results because the status quo is in no position to allow for needed change and the forces behind change cannot stand for the status quo.

But change and advancement cannot be stopped. The Church unsuccessfully tried to hold back the forces leading to the Age of Discovery. The initial signs of the First Industrial

Revolution put the order of Absolutism on a death watch. The logjam caused by the decentralized societies of Self-Determination would be cleared by Nationalism in order to make way for the Second Industrial Revolution. The need for globalization and the creations from the Space-Digital Age ultimately forced the Superpowers to tame Nationalism. It should be clear by now that human advancement will not be confined by the boundaries of an out-of-date world order.

Also becoming evident by now is that the seeds of each productivity boom in the succeeding world order are sown in the preceding one. Or, to borrow Mr. Jobs' words above, the dots are established in one world order and are connected in the following. So to have an idea of what the next world order might look like, it would be useful to ask what today's seeds are. What has been sown in our time, or is being sown, that will ultimately – once the impediments are cleared away – yield the fruit of the world's next great productivity boom?

In the previous chapters, the most prominent impediments were identified. The first was the world's current energy platform with its dependence on carbon, the second was the sectarian governance of the Middle East, and the third was the economic imbalances caused by uncontrollable globalization. What will it take to remove these impediments and what will be the resultant characteristics that will attach to the leaders of the next world order, the characteristics that will come to define it?

For one thing, a new world order will undoubtedly embrace the *technology* of these times and improve upon it. Since every new world order builds on foundations laid in the previous, it's reasonable to assume that the successful societies of the next world order will possess significant technological sophistication. Limited not only to gadgetry, the new technical knowledge will achieve the most efficient methods of gathering huge amounts of information and making sense of it. Today, we can gather it. But managing it, securing it, deciding what it all means and how to act upon it – these have all been a bit more challenging. Most likely, the future world order leaders are highly developed technologically even now, creating for themselves a head start for the potential conflict with those who will strive to maintain the status quo. Technological advantage will help win the conflict and then help enforce the ensuing peace.

Technology, of course, encompasses communication and the leaders of the new order must therefore possess *dominance of the world's communication infrastructure.* This means dominance of space. Information and communication technology is, and will continue to be, developed alongside space technologies – satellites and spacecraft. Developments in navigation and robotics, along with nano-satellites and micro-satellites, and continued connectivity and networking – a powerful grid of space-based technology – will define the communications infrastructure of the future. Of course, it will need to be defended, maintained, and improved upon. The world's new communication infrastructure must be free from potential threats and, therefore, space will need to be controlled by the next world order's leaders.

A new order will be led by those with *world-class leadership abilities.* This might seem self-evident but it has eluded despots throughout history, those who sought dominance within a world order but whose plans were ultimately thwarted. Hitler, Stalin, Saddam Hussein – these are the faces of narcissistic psychopathy. Despots of this grade are followed only for short periods of time and never achieve the complete dominance they set out for. Ultimately, they are brought down by the rest of the world. Global leadership requires the willingness of the world to get on board for wherever the new leaders are going. The majority of the world's population will never be inclined to follow a tyrant. Thankfully, it is, in fact, during times of chaotic tyranny that great leaders do appear. The great leaders seem to possess a prophetic and uncanny knack for sensing the world's direction. Bismarck and Lincoln foresaw Nationalism. FDR foresaw the reign of the Super-powers. And these were not exceptions. In virtually every century can be found at least one, and usually several, eminent leaders whose greatness appears at the cusp of world change. Without delay, they confronted the impediments. With spot-on foresight, they executed their vision of the future world order. These notable leaders, using the impetus of change, were able to gather the necessary momentum to lead their societies through the turmoil of world order transformation. Whether or not they realized their actions would be the bases for world order change is debatable but the success of selected societies in every developing world order has been, and most surely will continue to be, very much dependent on visionary leadership.

This characteristic of leadership presupposes a wide-spread culture to lead with an easily manageable *language.* It's unrealistic to imagine the bulk of the world suddenly switching gears and attaching itself heart and soul to that which is not familiar to it. The world has been moving toward adopting Western ways and the English language for over three hundred years now, a trend that is not likely to change direction over the relatively short span of time of the next world order change. Almost 20% of the world's population has at least a working knowledge of the English language. English is now the dominant language for politics, science, law enforcement, and international businesses like banking, oil, and travel. Most of the senior military officers in the G20 nations are proficient in English.

It's difficult from a Western standpoint to even imagine the difficulties that China faces, for instance, with its 8 primary dialects and over 250 languages, many of which are mutually incomprehensible to each other. And this doesn't even include the complexities of the written languages where individual characters can represent one syllable, or a word, or a part of a polysyllabic word. Chinese literacy requires the memorization of thousands of individual characters. China has been moving toward language standardization with the promotion of Mandarin, but naturally there is resistance from the cultures that speak the other dialects. Even in China, the popular trend seems to be moving toward learning English with almost a fifth of the population currently having some understanding of it. Fifty years ago the knowledge of English was negligible. Emphatically, this doesn't mean that the Americans or British will automatically be the leaders of the next world order. The position of new world order leader must be earned and will not be automatically bestowed on any nation. But it does mean that the leaders of the next world order must lead a significant English-speaking, Westernized culture, a circumstance that cannot be ignored.

Another cultural influence that will impact the next world order is the principle of *human rights* and individual freedoms. The world has traveled too far down this path to turn around. From as far back as the Renaissance and the Protestant Reformation, human rights have held a major place in the civilized world, evolving over years and becoming a major impetus for the advancement of humankind. There has been backsliding from time to time but only temporarily and generally for ostensible national security reasons (the Japanese internment camps during World War II, for instance, or certain NSA activities presently). But particularly in the years since the fall of the Iron Curtain, human rights have become almost a given for a majority of the world and it's difficult to envision the majority agreeably allowing them to be curtailed to any significant degree and for any length of time.

This respect for the individual and freedoms thereof

must include *religious freedoms*. In the West, theocracies began to die out over four centuries ago with the slow demise of the Holy Roman Empire and the worldly control of the Catholic Church. Religious divisiveness has continued and will continue probably as long as humans have spiritual beliefs, but government dictated *by* religious belief has been surpassed. The Middle East, laboring in the dictates of a world order that passed over four centuries ago, will see the eventual abandonment of its oppressive theocracies in favor of the religious freedoms and human rights that its people will demand.

By definition, individual rights also mean some form of *capitalistic economic system*, with freedom to buy and sell in an open marketplace of products and services and ideas. A new world order, as we know from history, will allow for the rise once again of tremendous productivity. But this must be fueled by a system that is accommodating to the idea of capital formation with efficient markets determined by risk and reward, free of manipulating intervention. There must be opportunity – opportunity to succeed, yes, but even the opportunity to fail and try again. During the last fifteen years, with all the financial crises, capitalism has received a black eye. But this is typical during the end of a world order. Movement away from capitalism always happens when financial inequality reaches extremes. After the new world order is in place and the financial inequality is resolved, the leading societies will again move back toward free-market capitalism. There is no way around the fact that free and fair markets with privately controlled capital are the most efficient systems to allocate economic resources during a stable and productive environment. And very few complain about capitalism when widespread wealth creation is occurring in a representative form of governed society.

Capitalism coupled with technology will allow for the *advanced financial system* required for the new world order.

If the new order arrives by widespread world conflict, there will be significant rebuilding needed on all sides. Required will be a twenty-first century version of the Marshall Plan in which the U.S. helped rebuild Europe after World War II. The world will need to be able to get back on its feet and only a sophisticated economic infrastructure will allow for this. There are many inadequacies with today's global financial system. The structure will need to be overhauled just as it was during every other world order change.

The rebounding economy of a new world order will allow for *widespread opportunity*. Progress will come either by a wiping clean of the world's debt or the increase in productivity will simply erode it away. The attendant wealth creation will mean that extremes in financial inequality will smooth out. The general population will be presented with new ways by which to seize potential for economic growth. The restlessness and angst from today's continued divergence between those who control the lion's share of wealth and those who struggle for its morsels will dissipate.

History demonstrates that world order changes result in great wars of attrition which tend to be massive and long. In such an event, the likely victors will of necessity have control of *abundant resources*. This abundance is what was lacking with Great Britain in the fall of the colonial world order as the colonists sought control of the resources being developed in their own land. The abundance was lacking with the South during the Civil War as the industrialized Union Army stampeded through Virginia, Georgia, and the Carolinas in the final months of the war. The abundance swung from French to German control as the resources of the Rhine River regions of Alsace and Lorraine gave the newly unified German states dominance over France during and after the Franco-Prussian War. Germany would lack such abundance after World War I, gain it back, and lose it again during the course of World

War II. Japan would suffer defeat caused by a lack of resources as well. Of course decisive victory in a war could swing the balance of resources one way or the other. Those lacking at the beginning of the conflict could gain as the conflict proceeds. Either way, the winner will have control of the resources necessary to rebuild the world after such conflict.

It's reasonable, incidentally, to wonder whether the resources the world depends on now will be the resources relied on going forward. Given the current energy quandary, for example, is it practical to believe that oil will continue to be the world's dominant fuel? Today's energy paradigm is a world vulnerability begging for a resolution. If the world moves toward less carbon fuel and more electricity, emphasis will be placed on battery technologies, which would require vast amounts of rare earth elements. Interestingly enough, China currently controls more than 90% of the world's REE production and they have been manipulating export and production. Alternative sources of the minerals include Australia, Brazil, Canada, South Africa, Tanzania, Greenland, and the United States, but the production in these countries is small relative to China. REE mines around the world were closed and production was halted when China undercut the world's prices in the 1990s. As the world has become more and more dependent on China as the primary source of these minerals, China has been restricting exports, causing the world's supply to be uncertain and prices to increase. The EU, U.S., and Japan filed complaints with the World Trade Organization in 2012 regarding the manipulation of REEs. China's response was that production levels were significantly reduced due to environmental concerns. The world has been put on notice that alternative sources for this new precious commodity need to be developed. As mentioned, huge deposits of REEs have been discovered recently in Afghanistan, but also in North Korea. This could make the situations in these countries analogous to that of Saudi Arabia's situation with its oil. Will all of this go into the calculus when determining the next world order and resolution of the energy and Middle East dilemmas? Of course it will.

Additionally, a new world order cannot be won or maintained without *supreme military strength*. With the high likelihood of conflict ushering in the new world order, it will rise from the ashes on the backs of the conflict's winners. But it will collapse upon itself if not enforced. Indeed, it won't be worthy of being *the* new world order if it cannot be maintained. This military strength will require a larger societal commitment. Increased military spending will be needed. Most likely, a military draft will be needed as well. The nations carrying the new order will only be able to do so through the shared sacrifice of all of the members of those nations.

Most importantly, the new world order will be forged by the society that has the *character, willingness, and fortitude* to persevere through the inevitable darkest hours that accompany world order changes. Through the transformation, there must be a stable underpinning, a constant the people can rally around. An ethical base, not a "moral majority" based upon religious or spiritual beliefs, but a widely held conviction to do the right thing and act with principle. The society that builds the new order will do so only by drawing on its strength of character and its legacy of doing that which is right and proper. Only an order encompassing all of these characteristics will be able to resolve the impediments that are dragging the current order into stalemate and increasing volatility.

The world cannot operate effectively under hegemony. Nor is it realistic to assume that a one-world government can be operational with all the various competing self-interests. And yet the globalization of today's world is a bell that cannot be un-rung. The world will remain connected in the next order, even if it becomes disconnected for a time during the process that will get it there. Consequently, the next world order cannot be one reminiscent of, say, Nationalism, with power spread among a multitude of countries with no central governing authority making sure there is a free flow of ideas and commerce.

Also, the world cannot again be defined by two competing superpowers dividing a world that remains intent on unifying. Therefore, the next world order will most likely operate within defined *spheres* of regional power – the Americas, Asia, and Europe. Resources, markets, economies, culture, and defense will all be centralized around these spheres. Connectedness will continue, even if it's more regional in scope than global. Inter-regional connectedness will be channeled through the regional powers.

None of this is to suggest that a new world order will be a utopia. After every world order change, there are painful adjustments, even with the new opportunities. Those who held onto and fought for the continuance of the prior world order (Superpower) or even the one prior (Nationalism) will fail, be physically devastated, and then forced to comply. The new order will not come to them easily, notwithstanding even the best of intentions on the part of the victors. New orders come in on rocky ground. Large political issues may be settled but smaller ones abound. The American Revolution ostensibly decided the fate of taxation without representation, but just eight years after the Treaty of Paris, the new nation's first president had to send an army to western Pennsylvania (Washington himself rode at the head of the army) to quash a rebellion over the federal taxation of whiskey. Reconstruction attempts of the South after the Civil War were largely failures. The United States economy rose substantially after World War II, but Germany and Japan had to be rebuilt from scratch. Even many of those on the winning side of the war were economically broken. Great Britain spent her national treasury on the war and spent several of the post-war years in an "Age of Austerity."

In time, the world will right itself once again. The world will possess the characteristics that define a new order, creating the climate for another era of remarkable human advancement. History shows this. But history also shows the terrible cost, paid by the blood of millions. And this begs a perfectly natural question, asked either hopefully or still skeptically: Is there room for belief that the sequence can be broken? Is there a possibility that *this* time around, humanity can avoid its seemingly inevitable rendezvous with destiny? Is there a possibility of a reprieve from global war?

Is there a last hope?

CHAPTER EIGHTEEN

The Last Hope

Those who cannot remember the past
are condemned to repeat it.
GEORGE SANTAYANA

I've got news for Mr. Santayana: we're doomed to repeat the
past no matter what. That's what it is to be alive.
KURT VONNEGUT

This book opened with a question, namely, is there a cyclical pattern to the affairs of humankind? Is there something about the progression of the human race that inevitably leads it through recurring periods of war and peace? Is there a common thread that runs throughout human history, something that weaves it together into an identifiable pattern?

It would certainly seem so. Over the last five centuries, four major world orders – the Church, Absolutism, Self-Determination, and Nationalism – have fallen and another, the Superpowers, is on its deathbed. The transition from one order to the next has always, without fail, been forged in a terrible period of global conflict. As chaos abates, a period of tremendous productivity and wealth creation follows. This has happened in every case. But the period of productivity also ends, resulting in worldwide financial crisis due to massive credit bubbles. Financial inequality ensues along with volatile divisiveness and political factionalism leading to the evolution of the next world order with its attendant period of global conflict. This pattern has repeated itself with what must be regarded as unmistakable regularity.

Like life itself, world orders run in a cycle. They begin from the ashes of the old order, they prosper, they fail, and they ultimately expire, making way for a new order. But new world orders don't just replace old world orders. They replace those that have become dysfunctional. The world structure that evolved from the Superpower order could never have replaced the structure under Nationalism when it was at its zenith. The Superpowers replaced a cancerous Nationalism. Put another way, Self-Determination could not have worked during the age of the Church and the Church order could not have worked in the age of Nationalism. During any specific time of human history, there is a particular way in which the world functions best – that is to say in terms of humankind's creative process – and that way presents itself to the exclusion of all others.

To say that world orders have come and gone, along with the way the world has operated under each respective order, is not especially earth shattering. Most would understand this from their history textbooks. But what's remarkable (and overlooked by historians, as well as by political theorists and economists) is the correlation between the life cycles of the world orders and the periods of great human productivity, wealth creation, and subsequent burnouts. And, of course, the ramifications of those burnouts. At those moments, the dysfunctional world order can no longer produce the welfare required by humankind. The status quo embodies the impediments to further advancement and wealth creation, and must therefore expire and be replaced. But change never occurs easily because power is vested in the status quo, and the status quo has a natural interest in preserving itself. Change, therefore, never happens quietly. When the world moves away from the dying world order, there is no going back. Anarchy becomes the ensuing condition, though the status quo will always attempt to resolve the anarchy and maintain authority. But these attempts can never hold for long because the way the world now operates is flawed at its most fundamental level; the existing world order no longer works.

In the face of all of this comes a perfectly natural question: Might there be at least some hope that this theory of a sequential nature to humankind – with its inevitable global conflict at certain, regular intervals – is in error? Or if not in error, that the sequence can somehow be broken? For the stakes are high. True *global* war, as history recounts, is staggering in its tragic potential. The combined number of deaths for all the participating countries in World Wars I and II was close to eighty million. Deaths for the United States were over half a million. Factoring in the number of wounded and the number who served, there was hardly a family that was left unaffected by the world wars. Global wars are relentless in their propensity for inclusion. It seems no one gets left out. Sacrifices are made from every corner, from every city and small town and neighborhood.

The enormity of the stakes demands further scrutiny. Does the sequence mean that humankind's nature is utterly unchangeable? Are we but fish in a stream, trying to direct our course by fins and tail but ultimately yielding to the ineluctable flow of the current?

A forthcoming period of global war would presuppose

that we are, in fact, at the end of a world order. The Superpower order forged in the prior century has gone, or is going, the way of the Nationalism order before it, the order of Self-Determination before that, Absolutism before that, and the Church order before that. To restate the arguments here, or to put any finer point on the clearly observable set of circumstances the world finds itself in today, would be superfluous. A more relevant question might be whether a new world order can arrive in peace, with the old order departing quietly. Is there any room for thoughts of dramatic, world-altering change coming about without war? History does not seem to allow it. The Church order died in a three-decades-long war. The death of Absolutism required nothing less than revolutions. The death of Self-Determination required a civil war in the U.S. and contemporaneous wars throughout Europe. Nationalism ended in not one but two world wars. Can it be believed that the Superpower order will not require the same kind of violent force to be ultimately unseated?

Realistically, there are but three outcomes related to this seemingly inescapable sequence of humankind. First, of course, is that the theory is correct. There is an identifiable pattern of global conflict that humankind cannot escape. Second, yes, maybe the sequence has existed, but the evidence is purely circumstantial and the connections are not causal and have all been merely coincidental. The linkages between boom times and subsequent busts and financial inequality and structural impediments and global divisiveness and world war are all just so much unconnected happenstance. Finally, though the general concept may be valid, previous instances of something are nevertheless insufficient indicators of what will happen in the future. It's the inherent problem with inductive reasoning. Just because the sun rises every day, it's not a given that it will necessarily rise tomorrow.

It must be acknowledged that a belief in the second possibility – that there is no connection – is difficult to realistically maintain for long. It's not just that the historical evidence is circumstantial. It's that it's circumstantial and massive. The points along the sequence are not there by accident. Causal links are too obvious to ignore. High productivity burns out and is never immediately followed by a new period of high productivity. The consequence is always debt. Debt grows and the consequence is financial inequality. Financial inequality grows and the consequence is divisiveness. Divisiveness festers and the consequence is political polarity. Political polarity spreads and the consequence is revolution and war, which ultimately leads to peace and a clean slate. And productivity begins anew. The connections are unmistakable.

The primary hope for the second possibility might be this: while it has never happened in the past, maybe huge periods of productivity actually can come back to back. Maybe something can come along this time to reignite productivity and opportunity to sufficient degrees that the world's debt can be paid and the extreme financial inequality can be resolved. A technologically productive *something* – a silver bullet or a white knight – arrives on the scene prior to the point of no return. But of course the problem with this argument is that such an epic deliverance would have to be widely acceptable to both the power of the status quo and the power of change. Nations entrenched in today's technology would have to willingly restructure their economies based on the new technology, and at a cost they can no longer afford to pay.

Moreover, where is the impetus for development of new technology? There will come along nothing that will focus development quite like global war. This is not a justification for war, of course, but it is an undeniable byproduct of it. When life and death struggles take place between the most advanced powers of the world, such as what happens at the end of world orders, history shows that the competition for new technology is at its peak. The brightest, wealthiest, and most populous nations go to war, either to secure a new vision for the world or to hang on to the status quo, and the result is world-changing technology, the likes of which cannot be rivaled during times of relative peace (except for those times that immediately follow war). At such times of global conflagration, when the status quo is crumbling, nascent technologies that were previously obstructed now rise up to aid the cause of war. The world is flat no longer. Steam-powered ironclads replace wooden man-of-wars. Railroads make way for airplanes. The technology exploited by war becomes an indispensable part of the growth that follows in the ensuing peace.

A regional war throughout, say, Africa, would never be able to produce the same type of new technology as a multi-theater global war that would count as its participants the United States, China, Russia, and Europe. Battlegrounds throughout the Middle East and Africa and parts of Europe (perhaps the South China Sea? perhaps North America?) would, out of necessity, foster technologies as yet unseen. The largest asymmetrical warfare to date would require extreme strategies to deal with Middle East terrorism, cyber attacks (from China? from North Korea?), nuclear threats (from Iran? Russia?), or all three. Absent this driving force for technological innovation, where, in a stagnant world of crushing debt laden with the inertia of the status quo, will humankind's next period of great advancement come from? Where will *any* significant advancement come from?

This, then, brings us to the third possibility. The potential fallacy of inductive reasoning. Can hope be found here? Is the historical sequence truly an adequate indicator of future events? Is a global conflict a foregone conclusion based on humankind's past experiences? To answer this, perhaps the best we can do is estimate the likelihood. Is it reasonable to believe – is it more likely than not – that the sequence will continue the way it always has? And if not, why not this time?

It can be presumed that the popular answer to the why not question would run something along the lines of humankind having simply evolved beyond the horror of global war. This is the twenty-first century, after all, and we're all very connected now. Today's world could not possibly descend into the madness of global warfare. The motivation for such a belief is understandable. As human beings, we must unconditionally hope that a valid counter-argument to the inevitability of global conflagration exists in spite of all the persuasive reasons that tell us otherwise.

But if war is unthinkable to us, so it was for those who came before. We naively believe that we somehow understand the horrors of war better than they. Consequently, we'll find ways to avoid it, making whatever other sacrifices are necessary. But will we? And are the sacrifices war requires truly understood or will the world (once again) underestimate them? The timing of the sequence – with global war coming roughly four or five generations apart – is notably significant. Between the periods of world conflict, institutional memory recedes. Opaque remembrances tend to accentuate the glory and dismiss the pain. The World War II generation is dying off. There are roughly only a million U.S. veterans left from the original sixteen million who served in uniform. There are no World War I veterans remaining. American institutional memory today recalls war in terms of, say, Desert Storm or U.S. action in Afghanistan. Even Vietnam (58,000 American deaths) is only recalled firsthand by those over fifty. "It is well that war is so terrible," Robert E. Lee reportedly said in the midst of the Civil War. "Otherwise we would grow too fond of it." But global wars seem to come about once a century, with enough time in between to forget just how terrible they are. Yes, war is unthinkable. Until such a time as when the unthinkable becomes mainstream. And then, the course of human events shows, the unthinkable happens.

And yet the argument for humankind's evolution beyond war persists, actually gaining prominence in the second half of the twentieth century as the new era of globalization was sweeping the planet. Termed "Liberalism" by political scientists, this theory of international relations considers cooperation to be the motivating force behind the way in which countries deal with one another. It's a theory realistic enough to acknowledge that the world can be a dangerous place, but it presupposes that war is in nobody's best interest and geopolitical decisions are made with a sense of diplomacy. If power is needed, it can be wrought by means other than military, usually economic. But since the term liberalism connotes a departure from contemporary thought, and Liberalism in international relations theory has often been the contemporary thought of record, a better word might be Idealism, a term, in fact, frequently used to describe a particular subset of Liberalism. Idealism holds that geopolitical decisions ought to be made not just with a sense of diplomacy but with a sense of morality, and what is in the best interest of the state ought to be measured by what is in the best interest of other states.

There is, of course, an opposing view to Idealism in international relations theory. The counterbalance is Realism. Realism recognizes that sovereign nations, in order to survive, will take the view that they are under no obligation to act in any interest other than their own. There is little morality other than the moral imperative of self-preservation. Additionally, the gain or loss of power among nations is a zero-sum game whereby power gained by one country is offset by a loss of power by others. Under Realism, national survival is used to rationalize the ends at whatever the means. Realism in the extreme might have best been expressed by Niccol Machiavelli (1469-1527), whose work (especially *The Prince*) gave rise to the term "Machiavellianism" to describe government authority that uses brute force, deceit, outright warfare, or whatever other tools it deems necessary to ensure its own survival. The powerful will always prevail over the weak.

Realism and Idealism are not necessarily models for how countries should act, but rather they attempt to explain how countries *do* act. They're not guideposts or value markers so much as tools by which nations can interpret how their fellow nations may respond to any given geopolitical event. And both theories are correct, but only at particular times. One can find moments in history when Realism seems most credible. The unification of Germany in the second half of the nineteenth century is such a moment. The unification was made possible by the series of wars engineered by Bismarck with little respect for consequences outside of what was in greater Germany's best interests. One can also find stretches when Idealism seems a better description for international relations. The years following the Peace of Westphalia (1648) provide an example. The Peace ultimately established the modern concept of the state. The Congress of Vienna (1814-1815) was another attempt to provide a long-term peace for Europe after the Napoleonic Wars. In both of these cases, a balancing of power was achieved and war was (hopefully) considered a thing of the past. It's not difficult to see a parallel here with the state of the world following the Second World War (even the First, after the establishment of the League of Nations).

The history of the last five centuries reveals that Idealism seems more relevant than Realism immediately following a period of global conflict, with the beginning of a new world order. Realism, on the other hand, seems more relevant when existing world orders begin to die out and the world moves ever closer to the next period of global conflict. It's easy to imagine, therefore, that problems can occur when Idealism, because of unrealistic hope, is held onto long past its relevant usefulness. This can lead to nations anticipating the behaviors of other nations incorrectly, setting their geopolitical strategies by flawed assumptions.

Both theories – Realism and Idealism – suffer from a presupposition that the way in which nations interact is static. In fact, the way in which nations act is often driven by circumstance. What drives each theory is always the belief that what is happening at any given moment is representative of what is going to continue to happen. One looks at the world and constructs a theory to explain it. It is a perfectly natural thing to want to do. With a valid, enduring theory, it is hoped that policy can be made, stability can be achieved, and humankind's productivity can continue. Unfortunately, as history has demonstrated, dramatic change is the one human constant. Any useful theory of international relations has to account for the fluid nature of humankind's path through time.

What governs that path most significantly is humankind's access to wealth, the end result of being able to capture the output of creation. When there is abundant wealth and opportunity, there is one way in which nations interrelate and when there is not, there is another way. When world orders begin to fray, it is only the height of naiveté that can possibly allow for a view of the world from the dogmatic standpoint of Idealism. Nations in lethal danger are like people in lethal danger: they will do whatever they need to do to survive. As anarchy begins to spread, nations will seize whatever power they can grasp to try and stop the spread. And they will not be discriminating about whom they are seizing it from.

If today's Superpower world order is indeed on a death-watch, then interpreting international relations today would best be served by viewing the world through the lens of Realism. From this perspective, the impediments of today's world can now be considered anew to help determine the likelihood of averting a period of global conflict.

The vulnerability to world order posed by the chaos in the Middle East is the best place to start. For it is here that one major and intransigent point must be conceded by even the most idealistic of Idealists: the Middle East impediment will not be resolved without war. Of the three major vulnerabilities of our age, this one must be regarded as the least possible to be resolved peacefully. To do so would mean theocratic regimes relinquishing control of their governments peacefully. Authority based on Islamic fundamentalism would make way for more representative governments with freedom of religion. There would be more civil rights. Kings rich from oil would cede some of their power and wealth. Israel would be accepted. And Israel would allow for a Palestinian homeland. Hamas, Hezbollah, ISIS, and all the other terrorist organizations would freely lay down their arms. Iran would willingly forego its nuclear ambitions. Shia and Sunni conflict would cease. The world's addiction to Middle East oil would recede and the economies of the region would become less concentrated on oil as foreign investment would flood into the area to help with the region's economic diversification.

No rational person can believe even a small portion of this will happen. The region is a puzzle with no solution. Where is the peaceful way out of this? What can possibly be the world's response? The growth of large-scale radical movements throughout the Middle East with no national borders have made it difficult for the world's structure to respond. Power is shifting in erratic, dangerous ways. Countries are fragmenting before our very eyes. Sooner or later, the chaos will spill over outside the region in a cataclysmic way. To quote Yeats, the center cannot hold.

Is there, however, a way for a limited war – limited to the Middle East? This idea – the idea of a limited global conflict that will nevertheless eliminate the world's vulnerabilities and usher in a new world order free of those impediments – would mean not conflict between the major powers of the world, but cooperation. It would mean unparalleled collaboration between nations to – nonviolently – restructure the world's carbon energy platform while providing a soft landing for the Fall of the Rest and a solution to the dilemma of Western debt. Could it happen? The Middle East is a foregone conclusion, awaiting its resolution in brutal conflict. But is there hope that two of the three vulnerabilities can avoid such a fate? Does this idea represent a last hope?

Along with unprecedented global cooperation to restructure the global energy platform and to resolve the economic imbalances caused by unfettered globalization, subordination of self-interest must ensue. A worldwide coalition of sacrifice and austerity would be required. And of course this means much more than just political sacrifice at the government level. The individuals of every nation would have to agree to sacrifice and live with the hardships such a course would demand. Humankind, individual by individual, would have to ignore its inherent desire for self-fulfillment for however long it would take to restructure the economy of the world. Can this happen absent an event that threatens survival itself? Can nations and the individuals therein be moved to such sacrifice without the force of actual war?

On a national level, a single country perceived to be gaining an advantage would effectively break the required global coalition. Perhaps a handful of dominant regional powers would have to be selected to take charge of regulating the behavior of nations in their respective regions. World cooperation could be administered by and among this group in a format of world power sharing. Is this possible? Would the rest of the countries of the world follow along peacefully? If not, would the individual nations of the administering assembly support each other unconditionally? Would they support each other militarily?

Recognizing that the world's nations are now behaving in a manner consistent with Realism, it must be accepted that the steepness of this hypothetical climb, or any similar alternative, is for all intents and purposes impossible to overcome. Any alternative that requires global cooperation and global subjugation of self-interest requires a state of the world described by Idealism, a theory of international relations that should certainly by now seem completely incompatible with the world as it currently stands.

And there is another, more fundamental, more human problem. To believe any scenario that requires the kind of global sacrifice that would be needed to avoid war (a sacrifice, it might be argued, that may in the long term end up being even greater than the sacrifice of war) rests upon a willingness and ability to ignore not only the tide of history, but the reality of human nature. The concessions necessary by all sides are virtually impossible to imagine coming about voluntarily. Nobody will believe the concessions necessary. Nobody will believe the alternative – global conflict – can really happen, or, if they do believe it, that they themselves will be the ones on the losing side of it.

This is a time of geopolitical Realism. Nations – like they always have – will work for the good of their own self-interests. And human nature will take its course. George Santayana was right. But more particularly, so was Kurt Vonnegut. There is nothing that can stop the march toward global conflagration.

CHAPTER NINETEEN

The Crucible

To everything there is a season, and a time for every purpose under heaven...a time to kill and a time to heal...a time to mourn and a time to dance...a time to rend and a time to sew...a time to love and a time to hate; a time of war and a time of peace.
ECCLESIASTES 3

If the new order, in its configuration as described in Chapter 17, is capable of eliminating the world's current vulnerabilities and stoking once more the flames of human progress, it's worth considering at this point the price of that world order. World orders come at a horrific cost. They come in on nothing less than global conflict. The old order ends in a haze of chaos and confusion, born of the instability caused by the inescapable fact that man's productivity is anything but linear. Humankind's advancement comes in leaps and bounds, motivated at first by great necessity (the life-and-death stakes of war) and slowed by the subsequent lack of necessity and the inability of mankind to maintain a consistent pace in *any* human endeavor.

Nobody outside of despots and tyrants and dictators bent on world domination ever *wants* to go to war. And yet entire nations of people are moved to do so because, to put it simply, there is no other choice. World orders end because they must. The hallmark – the curtain call of the pervasive wealth-creation era – isn't noticed until it is too late. Man naturally falls into the trap of extending, in any way possible, the accustomed lifestyle rightfully earned during the upswing. When the productivity slows, man will resort to debt, believing that the economic pains being felt are being caused merely by some periodic, cyclical pause. But when the economic rulebook established by the world order has run its course, it is not a temporary pause. Unable to grasp this, man will continue to overextend, pushing debt to the point of financial crisis. It is not in the nature of man to recognize the state of affairs until the overextension is complete and can continue no further. Even if he could (somehow) recognize the impending calamity, he would be helpless in the face of it once the era of great productivity moves into its waning days and human nature starts to take its course.

Governments intervene, attempting to halt the true market forces at work, falsely believing that they can avoid the reconciliation of overextension. The hope is that a new wealth-creation era will come along to bail the world out. The boom times will return, it is thought, even though great periods of wealth creation have never come consecutively in humankind's history as far back as one wants to look. History also shows us that a new productivity epoch, such as the likes of the Industrial Revolution or Space-Digital Age, cannot develop without reconciliation of the debt burden.

With stagnating productivity and a reluctance to reduce living standards, the massive debt load cannot be unbridled and the result is even more debt, ultimately increasing until motivations born of self-preservation are forced upon every level of the global society. Rent-seeking becomes common-place as competition for the smaller piece of the world resource pie ensues. The burden is shifted and the resulting pressure is usually most felt by those who can least afford it, those who are incapable of competing against those who can. The growing level of economic inequality, a trend that started long before and moves in the opposite direction of the un-foreseen decrease in wealth creation, now moves toward the extreme.

Inequality forces divisiveness and conflict – the battle for the status quo begins.

People go to war. They can put it off. They can institute political and economic policies that essentially ignore the un-derlying lack of economic momentum and watch as conditions deteriorate to the breaking point. They can institute "beggar-thy-neighbor," self-preserving policies. They can try futilely to stem the tide of history. But they can only kick the can so far down the road. Ultimately, people searching for resolution do go to war.

World orders are operating codes and they die out when the code no longer fits the world's state of affairs or when the world begins to act in ways that contradict the code. The world under the monarchs worked well with its system of mercantilism so long as the code was followed, and that code was the implied contract between mother country and colony. The interests of the colony would be protected. King George, in financial jeopardy, violated the code with the burdensome taxation of his colonists. The code broke down. Suddenly, the world was without its rulebook, flailing about in a kind of anything-goes environment that bred new ideas, new possi-bilities for new rules, and inevitably a whole new code. It was happening with all the monarchies. In the throes of the end of the wealth-creation cycle, the world order stopped making sense. And when a sufficient number of the world's people abandoned it, something had to give.

The American colonists resolved the quandary of the monarchs, rewriting the code and introducing the world to the concept of self-determination. But they left one unresolved problem on the table: not everyone enjoyed self-determination. The issue of slavery never went away and in the next century, that bill would have to be paid. But for the Founding Fathers, the immediate issue was breaking with England. The compromise was worth it. This, too, is what happens in the ugly process of world order change. Every new house has some defect somewhere that is complacently overlooked at the beginning. But of course the imperfection stubbornly resurfaces as the house ages.

World order changes are always marked by attempts to resolve quandaries that cannot be solved by least bad answers. A twentieth century example of this: During World War II, in November of 1939, the Soviet Union bombed Helsinki. Finland was at one time part of the old Russian Empire, declaring her independence in 1917 after the revolution. Now, the Russians wanted Finland back. The country was an important northern buffer for the ever-increasing threat from Hitler's Germany. The Soviets didn't exactly claim the action as such. Instead, they were, so went the official statements, annexing the country for the benefit of the "Red Finns" who resided there – those who wanted union with the U.S.S.R. The bombing galvanized Finland and the country fought back admirably in what became known as the Winter War. Ultimately, of course, they were no match for the Red Army and by March of 1940, they were forced into a treaty, surrendering much of their land to the Soviets.

But then Finland looked for help, finding it in a rather unpopular source: Nazi Germany. Germany was planning an offensive against the Soviets and an alliance with Finland proved strategic for both sides. Finland would break from the alliance eventually, but only when Allied victory over Germany seemed imminent, and only under pressure from Germany's enemies, including the Soviets who had, by 1944, agreed to a treaty with Finland in exchange for the Finns expelling the German army from their land. The Finnish strategy was reversed, in other words. Now, Finland was allied with the Soviet Union, fighting Germany in what would become known as the Lapland War.

This is what war (and the time that leads to war) is. It is messy and convoluted and it's often not until hindsight that one can see who the good guys are and who the bad guys are. Even then, it depends on one's perspective. History, they say, is written by the victors. New world orders lend credibility to them. There's not anything necessarily moral about it, though morality is what is frequently invoked in order to, first, fight and, second, to rationalize afterwards. It's estimated that under Joseph Stalin's regime, more than ten million people were killed at his direction. Between Hitler and Stalin, whom should Finland have allied itself with? The question can only be answered in the way Finland answered it and the way in which every country answers such questions: you ally yourself with whoever will help you maintain your sovereignty and way of life. For Finland, that was Hitler's Germany at one point, and Stalin's U.S.S.R. at another.

During these times of world transformation – the murky gray times in between world orders – things get ugly precisely because there is no functioning black and white authority. The League of Nations was set up as a potential new world operating code after World War I, but its ability to lead was doubtful from the start. Germany, Japan, Italy, and Spain would all withdraw in short order ("The League," said Mussolini, "is very well when sparrows shout but no good at all when eagles fall out."). World War II followed because the world lacked an authoritative code to follow.

Today, of course, the order of the Superpowers is gone. Where is today's operating code? Chaos reigns in the Middle East and elsewhere. Terrorists strike unchecked. Leadership is lacking both in ability and will, particularly by the one remaining superpower. Volatility and instability is commonplace. Countries can't determine whose side to be on for any given political issue nor how the United States will respond each time. The consistency in ideals that marked the Cold War is gone and what's left is confusion and opportunity for despots. Following the fall of the U.S.S.R., the first to come along was Saddam Hussein with his invasion of Kuwait in 1991, complete with the use of chemical weapons against Iraqi Kurds. This was followed by the Yugoslav wars of the 1990s, producing the most war criminals since Nazi Germany with the likes of Slobodan Miloševi , Radovan Karadži , and Ratko Mladi (the "Butcher of Bosnia"). In North Korea, Kim Jong-un, following in his father's footsteps, continues to create increasing insecurity for U.S. allies South Korea and Japan. The civil wars in Africa over the last two decades have left millions dead. Would Syria have degenerated into disarray in a world governed by both superpowers? Iran has continued and will continue to force its nuclear power aspirations on its foes in the region. Across the globe there are genocides, chemical weapons, nuclear arms, and dangerous non-state terrorists. The Cold War stayed cold. The world didn't go to war unless it involved the superpowers or was sanctioned by them. Today, the world is heating up and U.S. hegemony appears impotent in the face of it. The world lacks authority and direction.

It is at these times in history when the unimaginable becomes real. The institutional memory of the carnage experienced four or five generations prior has faded. The vigilance and deterrence maintained by the aging world order becomes lazy and repressed. Even in the face of perilous volatility, there remains an overconfidence and overreliance on crumbling safeguards. There's an arrogant and prevailing belief that man has evolved to a new level of humanity and prior evils have been exorcised. That belief, however, is held only by the leaders of the reigning world order. That the unthinkable can never happen again isn't a sentiment necessarily shared by those whose aim it is to unseat or destabilize the power structure within the dying order by whatever means may be required.

But if war is death, it is also rebirth. It is man at his worst, but it is also man at his best. Out of global conflict comes the advancement of the human race. The strongest and hopefully best ideas win out. While the world order is collapsing, a kind of smorgasbord of alternatives presents itself. But war is unforgiving. The weaker ideas run their course, some more quickly than others. It's a Darwinian process. The likes of imperialism, slavery, and extreme nationalism stubbornly hang on until they are bludgeoned into submission, becoming victims of a world order in which they cannot compete. It is as if the people of the world collectively speak, collectively decide who and what to follow. The tide of a new world order becomes an unstoppable force.

More than anything, humankind's finer virtues rise during periods of global conflict. As opposed to the peak times of productivity booms where mistakes and moral failings can go little noticed, there is no such margin for error when nothing less than survival is at stake. Societies are won or lost on the decisions of their leaders. The surviving world order will have been led by people who had great insight into the future, people who were uniquely adept at assessing the strengths and weaknesses of the masses, planning winning strategies, motivating the people, executing world-changing plans. Leaders will emerge or leaders will fail to emerge and each particular society will move forward for better or worse with the consequences. The world will be blessed with the likes of another Washington or Bismarck or Lincoln or Churchill or Roosevelt to guide it to the next step in humankind's history.

Of course society must follow. The momentum of the new world order must, in the end, be carried by the people. The likes of a Greatest Generation will step up, or the society will wither under the strain. The Southern aristocratic society during the Civil War, British society during the American Revolution, German society during World War II – in each case the society was unwilling to embrace the new, unwilling to let go of the old and choosing instead to die out with it.

Perhaps the process is best described as a crucible. Tested by fire and forged to withstand competing but corrupted philosophies, the ideals most worthy for the advancement of man evolve. Out of the fire, humankind is propelled into a new and promising direction. For the champions of the resulting new world order, productivity is ignited, the excessive leverage is resolved, and the trend of inequality is reversed. The losers, meanwhile, must be converted, to join in the new world order and share in the benefits.

Global conflict set off by a change in world order is this. It is a crucible. It will test and forge whatever is placed into it, and when world orders end, *everything* is placed into it. What remains is molded into the next world order. And the cost, terrible as it may be, is always deemed worth it. Ask the winners of the global conflicts that have preceded the new world orders – the creators of those new world orders.

Roughly every century, humankind must go through the crucible. It is a terrible thing. But it is as natural as the rain before the sunshine or the darkness before the new day. It is humankind's nature, unavoidable unless, as discussed, productivity itself is eliminated, a decidedly *un*natural proposition. An impossible one, really.

The natural universe persists in a cycle of death and rebirth. It should not be surprising that humankind's history does the same.

Legacy

It was the best of times, it was the worst of times, it was the age of wisdom, it was the age of foolishness, it was the epoch of belief, it was the epoch of incredulity, it was the season of Light, it was the season of Darkness, it was the spring of hope, it was the winter of despair, we had everything before us, we had nothing before us, we were all going direct to Heaven, we were all going direct the other way.
CHARLES DICKENS, *A TALE OF TWO CITIES*

The idea that the world is in a state leading to global war is terrible to contemplate and difficult to accept. Acceptance is frightening, as it ought to be. Acceptance doesn't mean letting go of one's fears. Fear can be useful, after all. Fear can inform and serve as a call to action. But we mustn't act *out of* fear. This is not a book intended to invoke panic. Think of it as a clarion call for what appears to be unavoidable. For those who disagree with the thoughts expressed in this book, think of it as a challenge. Is there an alternative future, a less bleak one? How might the unavoidable be avoided?

When the world comes out of the crucible better for it, as it will, it will have been led by those who have acted appropriately and in a deliberate, informed, confident way. This is what true leadership is about. And as discussed previously, the winners of the next period of global conflict will be the nation, or group of nations, that evolve as the most able to lead the world through the crucible. The new order will be led by those with *world leadership abilities.* These abilities do not include operating out of fear. History has consistently defeated those who have done so. The Hitlers ultimately lose.

The West and others who have adapted to the West's culture, the United States in particular, are in a unique position to lead the world into the next world order for the reasons detailed in Chapter 17. These countries have the resources, the reputations for leadership, the traditions of economic opportunity where anyone can work hard and succeed, systems of representative government, and legacies of human rights.

It is this last attribute that is, perhaps, the most important. Humankind operates under the presumption of free will. The ability to exercise this free will is fundamental to what it means to be human. Recall Maslow. People will inexorably move towards a state of self-actualization. We are, all of us, seeking lives of fulfillment and meaning. In our own unique ways, we each pursue that which gives our lives a sense of value and consequence. If we are not free to do this, if we are not free to realize this pursuit, we will combat that which is obstructing us. Our creative potential must and will ultimately be realized. This is the history of humankind. What happens when world orders begin to fail can be reduced to this: the ability of a great many people to exercise their desire to pursue meaning and fulfillment becomes impeded by the vulnerabilities of the age. *This* is what is truly at the root of conflict created by world order change.

There's a reason that the United States has persevered. It

was forged in one world order and has survived two others. Why? Because of its commitment to remove that which obstructs the unstoppable human movement towards higher self-actualization, at whatever cost. If the United States strives to lead the next world order, hopefully it will not be doing so to maintain some world order of the past. Colonialism, slavery, fascism, communism – all have been faced, all have been defeated. What has given America its strength through the years are its structure of government and a resulting system of leadership that has recognized that the winning side of every world order change has been the side that saw the need to remove the impediments of humankind's pursuit of self-actualization. It's no accident; it's no coincidence. The resolve of the U.S. is often underestimated in this regard, from both within and without. But the ideals and principles codified in its Constitution and the laws and structure that serve to underlie that resolve have proven time and again to be worth fighting for by those who have lived, and died, as Americans.

The pursuit of self-actualization is the unstoppable governing force of human nature. We move toward it unconsciously. Each world order change is a necessary correction, designed to take the world back to the state from which it has inevitably strayed – the state of relative freedom. The correction comes in with the power of a tsunami. Mark this well: to fight this unavoidable wave is to fight the very thing that makes us human. It has always been, and will always be, a losing proposition. When the world goes to war at the end of a world order, there are two sides. One hangs desperately on to the status quo; one moves away from it. The former side loses. King George III clung to colonialism. Louis XVI clung to absolutism. The leaders of the American South clung to antiquated society in their pursuit of self-determination. Hitler and Mussolini clung to imperialist nationalism. In each case, the world was evolving beyond these paradigms and in each case, these leaders could not see the evolution or chose to ignore it.

On the other side is the leadership of Washington. Of Lincoln. Of Roosevelt. Leadership that senses where the world is moving, where it must move. Leadership that understands what gives America her underlying strength, indeed her greatness. More than anything, she embodies that which is most human – the striving, the reaching, the inherent desire for growth and meaning. If America comes out of the crucible worse, it will be because of the lack of this kind of leadership.

And along with leadership comes the commitment and perseverance of those who share the ideals of the leaders. The citizens whose loyalty to the core principles becomes tested and then strengthened. In this way, the whole nation serves as a global example. If as Americans we lose our collective ideals, if we fail to take the lead in the subjugation of the world's stifling vulnerabilities, if we continue consuming beyond our means and burying our heads in the sand, if we fail to act or act from fear rather than conviction – then we will lose the global leadership position we hold. The world will look elsewhere and the consequent vacuum will be filled by a nation more deserving of carrying the world into the next order. America will become a second-rate country, a nation of followers playing a supporting role. If in the next world order, or two or three world orders from now, the relevance of the United States has been lost – it will not be because humankind somehow gravitated from the natural course it takes toward the exercise of free will and pursuit of meaning and fulfillment. It will be because the United States has instead shifted away from this course. It will be because the Constitution, with its separation of powers and its rights of the individual, has somehow lost its sacred stature.

Therefore – and this is most important – the new world order is for the United States to lose. Currently, much of the world is questioning whether America has lost its focus. Promises made have not been kept. Ambiguous messages are sent regarding the appropriate use of military force. Doubts over U.S. foreign policy have been expressed from the likes of the Philippines, Singapore, and Vietnam. The country has had to make repeated assurances to Israel and Japan that the United States stands behind them, assurances that have become necessary as the skepticism of American will and ethos has grown within the leadership of those nations. Coalitions of support for potential Middle East military action are harder to come by. Nothing less than the loss of world leadership is currently at stake.

I don't happen to think it's our destiny to lose the support of the rest of the world, at least for long. Leadership *will* emerge. The principles of our society *will* remain intact. The United States has a way of producing the right people at the right times, and our national sense of community in times of crisis enables us to rally behind those people. Leaders and followers, too, are forged by the crucible. In times of great crisis, we have a way of falling back to our roots, bolstered by our history, inspired by those who have come before. The World War II generation lost over 400,000 of its most promising young men in the European and South Pacific theaters of war; 600,000 more were wounded. The entire nation made monumental sacrifices. Their legacy is now our legacy. It is our inheritance. If we are indeed faced with the inevitable, we have a sacred obligation to carry the torch that has once more found its way to us. And we have a responsibility to the generations that come after us – our children and our grandchildren who will live free to pursue their own happiness in the world we must create and keep safe for them.

In the neighborhood where I grew up, there was a couple named Millie and Joe. Both had served in World War II. Millie was one of the Women Airforce Service Pilots – a WASP. Joe was a pilot, too, flying combat missions in the Pacific. Male pilots went to war but female pilots were often used to test planes and get them to where the fighting was. That's how Millie and Joe met. I remember as a teenager hearing them talk at neighborhood gatherings about the days of war and I was struck first by the nostalgia the two obviously felt for those times and, second, by the sadness. It was an interesting mix. They laughed as they told amusing anecdotes of people they had known. Millie would joke about how she actually outranked some of the combat pilots. But tears would well up when they told of people they had lost, people they would never forget. Through it all, I could sense their pride for their service and for what their generation had accomplished. "Those were some times," Millie would say. "Those were some times."

Years later, upon reflection, I would come to understand that Millie meant more than just good times and she meant more than just bad times. For the World War II generation – as well, I would suspect, for the generation that delivered this country and the generation that held it together in its weakest moment – the times were, to use Dickens's words, the best of times and the worst of times. It truly was the season of light and the season of darkness. A time of belief and incredulity. It was everything that humanity experiences and everything humanity stands for – the best and the worst – distilled into one epic moment. An earth-shattering moment. A world-changing moment. But in that moment rests a truth: the very truth of humanity. The truth of what it means to be a human being.

One way or another, when the smoke of the old world's destruction clears, a new era of great productivity and freedom will once again be upon us. The world's divisiveness will have been removed. Peace will reign. Inequalities of opportunity will have been leveled. The majority of people will be free again to exercise their will and chase their dreams. The world will once again be united, and the sun will rise on a new era full of promise. We must be prepared for this, too. We must lead through the conflict, and we must lead through the peace.

And we will remember the sacrifice of those who helped bring this world about. That remembrance, too, will be a part of our legacy.

And, in time, we will be required to do it all over again. Of course we will. Collectively, we identify the barriers to advancement and we set about removing them, however demanding the task. We survive. We move forward. But we never escape the sequence that is our lot, the progression that creates the barriers in the first place. It is our nature; it is who and what we are. It is the worst of us. And it is the best of us. Maybe that's our biggest inheritance and our biggest legacy. For we are human. Always human.

– The End –

ACKNOWLEDGEMENTS

The creative influences on a book are nearly infinite, leaving acknowledgements only for nearby and incomplete salutes. I am extremely grateful to everyone that has contributed to this effort, whether mentioned or not.

I must first recognize my ally and creative editor Jerry Payne. He is a wonderful man who travelled the same emotional road provoked by the *Crucible's* being. I am different, for the better, because of our shared journey. Reeling me in on my tangents and challenging the theory nearly every step of the way, he forced focus and clarity to my thoughts and writing. Jerry is my literary sensei. I can't imagine having worked with someone better. Thank you.

And Christine, my wife, my compadre. Christine shares with me her subtle strength, unwavering faith, and fire – all a great help when I become stuck in more than just writing. She brings balance. I am in awe of her childlike kindness, dramatically juxtaposed to the prospects of global war. Our bond is fascinating and I am forever grateful for our being drawn together. Because of our relationship, I now better understand my parents' eternal love for each other.

Then, the people who have helped bring the *Crucible* to life – Nancy from Wyatt-MacKenzie; Heather and Brenden, the creative forces behind Circletrianglesquare in Portland; and "Hey Joe," my friend from Joe Wilson Photography. All make for a very good team and a fun adventure.

And my great friend Kimberly, who for the past two decades has always believed I was better than I thought. Everyone needs a friend like her.

Finally, sincere thanks to Glenn, who may or may not recognize himself here. Short on faith, he was long on ideas and this book is better for his having reviewed it.

INDEX

CPSIA information can be obtained
at www.ICGtesting.com
Printed in the USA
LVOW07s0421110117
520520LV00001B/104/P